UNITED ARAB EMIRATES

David C. King

Marshall Cavendish
Benchmark
New York

PICTURE CREDITS
Cover photo: © Jon Arnold/Danita Delimont
AFP: 8, 29, 34, 36, 38, 40 • age fotostock/P.Narayan: 76 • age fotostock/Silman Snozyk: 66 • alt.type/reuters: 15, 17, 50, 52, 55, 56, 58, 60, 71, 73, 79, 81, 83, 85, 93, 98, 105, 110, 112, 113, 115, 119, 121, 122, 123 • Art Director's: 33, 120 • Audrius Tomonis: 135 • Besstock: 1, 3, 12, 16, 19, 22, 23, 35, 44, 47, 51, 64, 67, 74, 82, 86, 87, 95, 96, 102, 106, 107, 117, 124, 129 • Caro/Sorge: 49, 53 • Corbis: 4, 27, 31, 41, 59, 77, 97, 108, 118 • Don Klumpp/Getty Images: 30 • Dorling Kindersley/Getty Images: 25 • Focus Team Italy: 78 • James Davies Worldwide: 6, 7, 9, 11, 20, 114 • James L. Stanfield/ National Geographic Collection: 116 • Jason Laure: 103 • John Dakers/Eye Ubiquitous: 94, 99 • Kevin Nicol/ Eye Ubiquitous: 109 • Lonely Planet Images/ Izzet Keribar: 43 • Lonely Planet Images/ Clint Lucas: 54, 65 • Lonely Planet Images/ Phil Weymouth: 62, 68 • Lonely Planet Images/ Chris Mellor: 92 • MCIA/Thomas Khoo: 131 • Peter Hellyer/Hutchison Library: 21, 46 • Photolibrary: 57, 63, 88, 125, 127, 128 • Robin Constable/ Hutchison Library: 101 • Steve Raymer/National Geographic Image Collection: 42 • Stockfood/Marcialis, Ren: 130 • Tim Graham/Getty Images: 5 • Tropix.co.uk/ Christian Smith: 70

PRECEDING PAGE
Adolescent Emirati boys enjoying a quiet afternoon.

Publisher (U.S.): Michelle Bisson
Editors: Christine Florie, Stephanie Pee, Andrea Lee
Copyreader: Mindy Hicks
Designers: Cynthia Lee, Rachel Chen
Cover picture researcher: Connie Gardner
Picture researchers: Thomas Khoo, Joshua Ang

Marshall Cavendish Benchmark
99 White Plains Road
Tarrytown, NY 10591
Web site: www.marshallcavendish.us

© Times Media Private Limited 1997
© Marshall Cavendish International (Asia) Private Limited 2008
All rights reserved. First edition 1997. Second edition 2008.
® "Cultures of the World" is a registered trademark of Times Publishing Limited.

Originated and designed by Times Media Private Limited
An imprint of Marshall Cavendish International (Asia) Private Limited
A member of Times Publishing Limited

All Internet sites were correct and accurate at the time of printing. All monetary figures in this publication are in U.S. dollars.

Library of Congress Cataloging-in-Publication Data
King, David, C.
  The United Arab Emirates / David C. King
    p. cm. — (Cultures of the world)
  Summary: "Provides comprehensive information on the geography, history, governmental structure, economy, cultural diversity, peoples, religion, and culture of the United Arab Emirates"—Provided by publisher.
  Includes bibliographical references and index.
  ISBN-13: 978-0-7614-2565-6
1. United Arab Emirates—Juvenile literature. I. Title.
  DS247.T8K552008
  953.57—dc22   2006030237

Printed in China
7 6 5 4 3 2 1

CONTENTS

Diana Point at Al Jabal
Al Akkar region, Hajar
Mountains.

3

**A traditional *barasti*
house.**

INTRODUCTION

THE STORY OF THE UNITED ARAB EMIRATES (UAE) is one of the most remarkable rags-to-riches sagas the world has ever witnessed. Until Western oil companies unlocked huge deposits of oil in the 1950s and 1960s, this small desert country in the southeastern corner of the Arabian Peninsula was virtually unknown to the rest of the world. Most of the people coaxed a perilous livelihood out of the desert and the shallow waters of the Persian Gulf.

By the time seven small sheikhdoms, or emirates, formed the federation of the UAE in 1971, fantastic oil wealth was already transforming the new nation. In the space of less than 50 years the UAE has become a land of glittering cities, with towering skyscrapers, luxury hotels and beach resorts, magnificent shopping malls, and one of the highest living standards in the world. In spite of the fantastic pace of change, the people retain their traditional values of generosity, hospitality, and friendship.

GEOGRAPHY

ANY DESCRIPTION OF THE United Arab Emirates (UAE) has to be based on the impact of the oil boom that began in the late 1950s. Every aspect of life has been influenced by the oil riches, including its geography and people's relationship with their environment.

In the past people struggled to survive in the harsh desert environment. Today, oil wealth has changed their relationship with it. Before the 1970s, for example, the journey from Abu Dhabi City to al-'Ayn was a difficult 100-mile (160-km) trek across burning desert sands. Today, the trip is made on a six-lane highway with a constantly watered grass divide lined with palm trees, bougainvillea, oleander, and other flowering trees. Beyond that line of trees is another thick belt of trees that helps to hold back the desert sands.

Opposite: **Rub 'al-Khali, the Empty Quarter.**

Below: **The rocky barren landscape of the Hajar Mountains in Dubai.**

Dubai's Jebel Ali port is the world's largest manmade harbor with 67 berths.

THE LAND AND THE COAST

The UAE is made up of seven small emirates on the southeastern corner of the Arabian Peninsula. The emirates are bordered by Qatar on the northwest; with Saudi Arabia wrapped around the country on the west, south, and southeast; and by Oman on the southeast. All but one of the emirates are on the coast of the Persian (or Arabian) Gulf; the seventh, al-Fujayrah, faces the Gulf of Oman and the Indian Ocean.

This is a small country, covering an area of 32,000 square miles (82,880 square km), about the same size as the state of South Carolina. The population, which numbered only 180,000 when the federation was formed in 1971, grew to 2,602,713 by 2006, roughly the same population as the state of Nevada. This amazing increase in just 35 years was caused by the influx of people from all over the world, who were drawn by the opportunities created by the oil boom. Great numbers came from other Arab countries and from India and Pakistan, as well as Iran, the Philippines, and China, with smaller numbers from Europe and the United States.

Natives from the emirates, called Emirati, now account for only about 20 percent of the total population.

Roughly two-thirds of the country's land area is lightly shrubbed or sandy desert, with a narrow coastal strip that is semifertile, especially with irrigation. In the south the emirate of Abu Dhabi lies on the edge of the notorious Rub 'al-Khali, the Empty Quarter—the largest area of continuous sand in the world, covering an area of 250,000 square miles (650,000 square km), an area nearly as large as the state of Texas.

In addition to some fertile areas, large portions of the coast are composed of salt flats, called *sabkhah*, formed over several thousand years by wind eroding the sand dunes. The salt flats form a belt 200 miles (320 km) long along the coast.

The coast itself is a mixture of reefs, shoals, lagoons, and low-lying islands. There are more than 200 islands off the coast. Some are privately owned by the ruling sheikhs. There are no natural, deepwater harbors on the Persian Gulf coast of the UAE, but the country has worked around this by constructing artificial harbors. In addition, there are three good, natural harbors on the Gulf of Oman.

A cultivated wadi situated in the Hajar Mountains.

OASES AND WADIS

Oases are often perceived as backyard-size islands of green in an ocean of sand. Oases actually vary greatly in size, and some are surprisingly large. The UAE oasis of al-Buraymi, for example, includes al-'Ayn, a city of 200,000 people.

CROSSING THE EMPTY QUARTER

Emirati have fond memories of two English explorers, Sir Wilfred Thesiger and Bertram Thomas, who crossed the Rub 'al-Khali with Bedouin guides. Thesiger made two crossings, in 1946–47 and 1947–48, which were described in his famous book *Arabian Sands* (1959). He disguised himself as a Bedouin from Syria to make himself less conspicuous, and only his Bedouin companions knew his true identity.

Although Thomas is not as famous as Thesiger, he has the distinction of being the first Westerner to risk crossing the seemingly endless sands in 1931. In his book *Arabia Felix* (1932) Thomas describes the Rub 'al-Khali as "a vast ocean of billowing sands, here tilted into sudden frowning heights, and there falling into gentle valleys, without a scrap of verdure in view."

A few small mountain chains form the only other topographical features. The largest chain, the al-Hajar, has some peaks reaching 4,000 feet (1,200 m) in the UAE, and twice that height on the Oman Peninsula. The mountain regions were once important centers of civilization. Archaeologists have found the remains of prosperous towns dating back to 2500 B.C. and earlier.

These oases have been vital to desert survival for centuries, especially in the past, when a camel caravan might spend two weeks crossing a stretch of desert. In addition to al-'Ayn, UAE's oases include Liwa', a fertile crescent of more than 50 separate oases. In the past 30 years, water from desalination plants and more modern irrigation systems have helped to maintain the lush greenery.

Riverbeds, called wadis in mountain regions, have also been important farming regions for many centuries. The country's upland wadis support such crops as wheat, sorghum, and alfalfa, plus a variety of fruits, including mangoes, bananas, limes, and grapes. The UAE is one of the world's leading producers of dates, and date palms thrive in wadis and around oases.

THE SEVEN EMIRATES

In its brief history as a nation, the UAE has displayed a remarkable degree of unity. At the same time, however, each emirate retains its own unique identity. They also differ greatly in size, population, and geographical features.

Abu Dhabi is by far the largest of the emirates, covering about 30,000 square miles (77,700 square km), which is more than 80 percent of the total land area. The UAE's capital city, also named Abu Dhabi, is situated on an island connected to the mainland by a causeway. Much of the emirate's land is desert, but Abu Dhabi includes the major oases of al-'Ayn, Liwa', and al-Buraymi, on the border with Oman.

Abu Dhabi also holds more than 95 percent of the UAE's proven oil reserves. This has made it the dominant emirate, both politically and economically. The ruling family has used its position wisely, insisting that Abu Dhabi's wealth benefit all the emirates.

Dubai, the second largest emirate, covers about 1,500 square miles (3,900 square km). While Abu Dhabi dominates politically and in terms of oil wealth, Dubai has considerable oil revenue of its own and has been

View of the Dubai skyline along Dubai Creek.

Vegetables are grown in a greenhouse in the desert of Ra's al-Khaymah.

the commercial hub of the country for many years. It is regarded as the most modern and free wheeling of all the emirates.

Sharjah (also called Ash Shariqah), the third largest emirate at 1,000 square miles (2,600 square km), has been overshadowed by Abu Dhabi and Dubai, but it has changed a great deal in the past 20 to 30 years. The ruling family has used the shared oil wealth and its own small quantity of light-grade oil to modernize the city of Sharjah and to establish modern roads, schools, and health-care facilities. In spite of its 21st-century look, Sharjah also shows remnants of its long history in the form of ancient forts and watchtowers, including a waterfront lined with dhows, the traditional boats used for fishing, pearl diving, and trade.

Three tiny sheikhdoms, 'Ajman, Umm al-Qaywayn, and Ra's al-Khaymah, commonly called the Northern Emirates, cover about as much area as Sharjah. 'Ajman, the smallest, covers just 100 square miles (259 square km) between the Persian Gulf and Sharjah. Many pearl divers once sailed from its port, but today the port contains a long wharf used to repair boats that supply the UAE's oil fields. The fertile soil in the mountains of 'Ajman also make it a producer of vegetables and citrus fruits.

Umm al-Qaywayan, with an area of 600 square miles (780 square km), is the second smallest emirate, and it is also the least populous, with fewer than 40,000 people. During the heat of the day, the streets of its main town are practically deserted. The offshore island of al-Siniyyah is a wildlife sanctuary with large populations of nesting herons, as well as cormorants, turtles, and sea snakes, while the sea cows called dugongs swim in the shallow waters. Archaeological excavations show that people have fished and hunted there for more than 5,000 years.

Ra's al-Khaymah, which covers an area of 660 square miles (1,690 square km), is the most fertile of the emirates, with groves of date palms as well as grazing areas for sheep and cattle, and varied marine life.

Finally al-Fujayrah, the most remote of the sheikhdoms, is the only one facing the Indian Ocean. Its 1,000 square miles (2,600 square km), located to the east of Dubai, is connected to the rest of the UAE only by a few paved roads. There is a strong sense of history dating back through many centuries of sea trade. The mountains bordering the emirate drop off sharply to the coast of the Indian Ocean. In addition to spectacular scenery, al-Fujayrah has some excellent agricultural land and has become important for raising poultry and dairy cattle.

CLIMATE

The climate of the UAE is, for the most part, hot and humid along the coast and still hotter, but dry, inland. The average January temperature is 65°F (18°C). In July the average temperature is a scorching 92°F (33°C); it can reach 115°F (46°C) on the coast and 120°F (49°C) inland. In midwinter and early summer, winds known as the *shamal* blow from the north and northwest carrying unwelcomed sand and dust. Rainfall rarely measures more than 3 to 4 inches (75–100 mm) in a year. Not surprisingly, streets and wharfs are quite empty in the early afternoon, at least in summer, and construction workers do much of their work in the early mornings and evenings. The extensive planting of trees and grass, the creation of numerous parks and fountains, and widespread air-conditioning have made the cities much more comfortable.

PLANT LIFE

The country's plant and animal life is surprisingly varied, and the government's efforts to draw tourists makes use of this variety. The deserts are host to several endangered species, and efforts have been made to protect and expand these populations. In terms of plant life, many hardy varieties of tropical and subtropical trees and other flora have been added alongside the indigenous species.

The UAE has been celebrating Tree Week in mid-April every year since 1981. Among the trees commonly found in parks and urban greenbelts is the gulmohar, often called the *fleur de paradis*, a native plant from Madagascar, enjoyed for its orange and red blossoms. The portia tree, also called the umbrella tree, is also common. The tree has small yellow flowers and small apple-like fruit, which are used to produce yellow dyes. The wood and bark are used to make a red dye.

Other trees with practical uses include the frywood, whose bark is used in the manufacture of medicines. This tree has papery, yellow pods that noisily clack together. The margosa, also called the neem tree, produces hundreds of tiny yellow flowers. The blossoms, along with the leaves, roots, and bark, are also used in the production of medicines.

DATE PALMS: THE DESERT'S GLORY

The date palm is the UAE's most important tree, and for centuries it was vital to desert survival. The fruit it produced was a staple of the Emirati diet, and its trunk and leaves were used to make a variety of household items and small boats. (Most of these products are now made of metal or plastic.) Date palm leaves were also used to make *barasti* houses, which were common before concrete was available. A *barasti* house had a wooden frame and supports with walls, room dividers, and a roof made of palm leaves. The leaves were also used to make a four-sided wind tower at the top of the house, which directed cooling breezes into the rooms below.

Date palms are native to the region. The fruits they produce, which range in color from pale yellow to deep red, hang in large

clusters, often 3 feet (about 1 m) in length. The trees thrive in oases, where the water table is close to the surface. Ancient irrigation channels, called *falaj*, carry water from underground springs to date palm groves. These channels are now lined with concrete rather than stone.

There are more than 22 million date palms in the UAE, and the country hosted the Third International Conference on the Date Palm in February 2006. Nearly 200 participants from 35 countries attended the conference to explore and discuss ways of expanding date cultivation in all the world's desert regions.

Many grasses, bushes, and other low-growing plants thrive in the desert. These include the desert squash, desert hyacinth, firebush, and Sodom's apple. Coastal areas and oases have a variety of plants and grasses as well.

ANIMALS

Each small region of the UAE has its own unique animal life, including birds, reptiles, and a number of rare species of larger animals. One of the many surprises of this fascinating desert country is that it is a conducive place for bird-watching, an activity that many people participate in. The country's determined effort to increase parkland and green space has led to a steady increase in birdlife. An additional factor is that the UAE is situated on one of the planet's main migration routes. Up to 300 species stop over there on their way to or from Europe, Africa, and Asia.

In addition, both Dubai and Abu Dhabi sponsor organizations called Natural History Groups, which engage in spotting and recording information about birds. The groups are especially active in autumn and spring—the best seasons for bird sightings. Bird-watchers have spotted some 360 species nesting, migrating, or wintering. Safa Park, a few miles outside Dubai City, has proved to be an excellent site for the hobbyists. Of the 230 species recorded there, some are common, such as robin and thrush, but there are also gray shrikes, European bee-eaters, and many warblers, including the great reed warbler. Dubai Creek and the shallow lake attract pintail ducks and many waders. Beach areas and the islands draw yet more varieties, including plovers, herons, flamingoes, terns, and egrets.

A lone black swan mingles among a flock of flamingoes at Ras Al-Khor sanctuary in Dubai.

The name Abu Dhabi means "father of the gazelles." An Arab legend about three hunters tracking a gazelle relates that the animal led them to an island close to shore, where they started a town, which they named Abu Dhabi.

The ruling sheikh of Abu Dhabi is the owner of an island named Sir Bani Yas, which has been declared a nature reserve. Reflecting the UAE's determination to protect its wildlife, Sir Bani Yas has been instrumental in preserving endangered species, including the oryx and the Arabian leopard.

The desert is still home to several endangered species, including the Arabian gazelle, the sand gazelle, Thomson's gazelle, the scimitar-horned oryx, and the gemsbok. All of these rare animals are also protected in game reserves.

Several species that were once desert dwellers are now found primarily in reserves such as Sir Bani Yas. These include the lynx caracal, the Gordon's wildcat, and the striped hyena. A few species, such as the red fox and Blanford's fox, manage to survive even in extreme conditions. In addition, there are several insectivores—mammals that feed on insects. These include the shrew and several kinds of hedgehog. In additon, the UAE deserts are also host to several bat species, in particular the Egyptian fruit bat.

Not surprisingly, the desert environment is a comfortable habitat for many species of reptile. More than 50 varieties have been recorded in the UAE, including many kinds of lizard and gecko, which are more common than snakes. Snake species include the desert boa, the sand snake, the Arabian rear-fang, and the sand viper, which buries itself in sand up to its eyes and nostrils.

MARINE LIFE

The coastal people of this region have relied on fishing for centuries for food and their livelihood. The Persian Gulf is home to schools of mackerel, grouper, tuna, and others, as well as shark and occasionally whale. Recent marine surveys have shown that the UAE's waters may be home to more than one-third of the world's 80 species of dolphin and whale. An increasing number of dhow excursions take visitors on dolphin watches (although not yet on whale watches). One of the world's largest populations of dugongs, or sea cows, is also located there. These big, gentle creatures are related to the manatee, another endangered species found in the inland waterways of the United States.

There are a number of coral reefs off the coast. The colorful tropical fish living among the coral have made scuba diving a favorite UAE sport. The waters of the Persian Gulf and the Gulf of Oman are also home to nine different species of sea snake. More human-friendly reptiles include several endangered turtle varieties, such as the loggerhead, hawksbill, and the olive Ridley turtle.

Many species of dolphin thrive in the waters of the UAE.

HISTORY

THERE ARE TWO HISTORIES OF the United Arab Emirates: the entire history of the region for the thousands of years before the discovery of oil, and the history of the half-century since the oil boom began. According to many observers, no nation has changed more or faster than the UAE has since the oil began to flow. The earlier history portrays a long and colorful past and sets the scene for the story of the modern nation.

Opposite: **An old fort with crenellated tower and ruined walls in Sharjah.**

Below: **A Bronze Age tomb in Fujairah.**

Detail from the Umm an-Nar Tomb, c. 2500 B.C. in al-'Ayn.

PREHISTORY

Human groups have inhabited the area that is now present-day UAE for more than 7,000 years. Archaeological findings indicate that Stone Age people living there used simple tools for farming, growing crops of wheat, barley, and palm dates from 3000 B.C. They also raised cattle, sheep, and goat. There is also evidence that by 2500 B.C., camels were domesticated and were probably used in establishing inland settlements at wadis and oases. In addition, trade items such as pottery and copper were being shipped to the early civilizations of Mesopotamia. In other words a well-developed maritime trade was already an important part of the regional economy as early as 2000 B.C.

After 300 B.C., in the centuries following the death of Alexander the Great, what is now the UAE was part of a trade network linking the Mediterranean world, including ancient Greece and Rome, with the cultures of the Indian Ocean and Africa. At the same time, camel caravans, bearing goods such as frankincense, made their way north through Western Arabia, while the coastal communities continued to rely on maritime trade. The people of the region used dhows of all sizes to export such goods as pearls, wood, and limestone marble.

THE COMING OF ISLAM

Sometime after 200 B.C. tribes of Arab peoples began moving into the region that is now known as the UAE. Some settled in coastal areas, while others sought the fertile inland wadis and oases. Initially, the Arab tribes fought with other groups living there, who were probably of Persian descent. Gradually, over several centuries, the two groups merged, with the original settlers being absorbed into the Arab tribal structure.

The new religion of Islam swept through the region in the years after A.D. 630. The religion's founder was the Arab Prophet Muhammad. God's words, as revealed to Muhammad, are contained in the Koran (or Qur'an), the holy book of Islam. Allah, the God in the Koran, is very similar to the God in the Bible or the Torah.

The spread of Islam began during Muhammad's lifetime, and its expansion accelerated after his death, in A.D. 632. Over the next three centuries the religion spread across North Africa and Asia, reaching into India and the islands of the western Pacific. All of the countries of the Persian Gulf are overwhelmingly Muslim.

The Al Bidya Mosque in Fujairah dates back 400 years and displays the unique architectural style of the time.

Islam is the name of the religion. Followers of Islam are called Muslims. There are two main branches of Islam—Sunni and Shia. Most native-born citizens of the UAE are Sunni Muslims.

THE SHEIKHDOMS

Over the centuries various Arab tribes and their sheikhs came to rule specific areas. By the 1700s, for example, one tribe, the Bani Yas, controlled the town of Abu Dhabi and the oases of al-'Ayn and Liwa'. One branch of the Bani Yas, known today as al-Nahyan, continues to head the government of Abu Dhabi. People were loyal to their tribe and its sheikh, rather than to a place or a country. These loyalties remain strong today.

Similarly, the emirate of Dubai was established under another branch of the Bani Yas. Dubai, which had existed as a town before 1580, was built along the banks of its creek, which offered one of the best anchorages for ships in the region. Ships from Persia, Pakistan, India, and other countries used its wharfs; many crew members from these ships remained in Dubai and quickly assimilated into the increasingly multicultural coastal society.

The Northern Emirates were dominated by the Qawasim clan, part of the powerful Huwalah tribe. The Qawasim became a sea power in the 1700s, their growing strength a threat to Great Britain, which resulted in clashes with the powerful fleet of Great Britain. Another large and powerful tribal group, the Sharqiyyin, was spread across what is now al-Fujayrah. The followers of the sheikh eked out a living by fishing, cultivating date palms, and sea trading.

MARITIME TRADE

Trade between the Mediterranean world and Asia, including China, India, and the Spice Islands, developed during the eras of the Greek and Roman empires. Coastal villages on the Persian Gulf became midway stops in this long-distance exchange, and by the eighth century A.D., Arab dhows and seamen were becoming key players in the global game of trade.

After about A.D. 750 the Gulf trade brought great riches to the new Muslim Empire. The Arabian capital of Baghdad, in present-day Iraq, became one of the world's wealthiest and most famous cities. The seamen and ships of the Persian Gulf inspired romantic tales, such as the stories of Sinbad the Sailor from the Arabian Nights.

Being a maritime trader was hard and dangerous. The men spent months at sea, crammed onto open ships that were little more than floating cargo bins, with the crew living as best they could on top of the cargo. The Italian explorer Marco Polo was shocked to find that the planks of the dhows were not nailed together, but instead were stitched with twine made of coconut fiber. The construction, he wrote, "makes it a risky undertaking to sail in these ships. And you can take my word that many of them sink because the Indian Ocean is very stormy."

The merchants who succeeded in the maritime trade could make a fortune in a single voyage, and the ports of the Persian Gulf became great crossroads between Europe and Asia. Dubai and other Gulf ports added pearls and Arabian horses to a trade that included goods from India, such as cotton, spices, and swords; products from China, such as silk, porcelain, and tea; goods from the Middle East, such as carpets, muslin, and perfumes; and goods from East Africa, such as gold and ivory.

Many maritime traders, lured by the exotic goods found at the Persian Gulf ports, made ardous journeys on ships like this.

THE PEARLING INDUSTRY

The pearl diving industry was important to the Gulf sheikhdoms for more than 2,000 years, reaching its peak in the early 1900s, when more than 400 pearling dhows were based at Abu Dhabi, about one-third of the emirate's total fleet. An estimated 22,000 men were involved in the industry, a great percentage of the population at that time.

Diving for pearls was a grueling and dangerous occupation. The men were at sea for up to four months, during the hottest months of the year. They dove on empty stomachs to avoid cramps, and they faced the constant danger of attacks by jellyfish, sharks, and sea snakes. The work was sometimes very profitable, and this attracted men who had few other opportunities for work.

The industry was mostly destroyed in the 1930s, when the Japanese learned the secret of cultivating cultured pearls. The economic chaos caused by the Great Depression in the 1930s dealt an added blow.

COLONIAL RIVALRIES

In another effort to find a sea route to China and the Spice Islands, some Europeans tried sailing west across the Atlantic Ocean. Christopher Columbus was the first to try.

As the European kingdoms grew in power, their leaders and merchants were eager to control this fantastically lucrative trade. Portugal was one of the first to send its fleet to capture key posts in the Indian Ocean and along the coast of Africa and the Strait of Hormuz, in the 1500s. One hundred years later, they were driven out by the Dutch. The British and French attempted to secure key ports in the region in the 1800s.

The British did not want to establish colonies in the Persian Gulf, but rather to control the sea routes in order to safeguard their trade with India. The Qawasim tribe, in control of Sharjah and Ra's al-Khaymah, saw the powerful British fleet as an invasion force and put up stiff resistance, frequently attacking British ships throughout the late 1700s and early 1800s. The British retaliated. They blamed the Qawasim for the piracy that was interfering with trade on the Gulf. In 1819 the British attacked and burned coastal towns in the regions of Sharjah, Umm al-Qaywayn, and 'Ajman, destroying nearly all of the ships.

As the Qawasim's power declined, the tribal rulers of Abu Dhabi and Dubai rose to prominence. The al-Maktoum family set about making Dubai the leading trade center of the Gulf Coast, while Abu Dhabi emerged as the leader of the highly profitable pearling industry.

In 1835 under British pressure, the rulers of four emirates—Dubai, Abu Dhabi, 'Ajman, and Sharjah—signed a truce outlawing acts of war at sea during the pearling season. This agreement was turned into the Perpetual Treaty of Peace in 1853. In this unusual treaty seven emirates agreed to continue the ban on war at sea, and in return Great Britain agreed to protect them against external attack. From this time on the seven emirates were known as the Trucial States, and the British continued to defend them and manage their foreign affairs.

THE FORMATION OF THE UAE

The British agreement with the Trucial States helped to fend off other powers, especially France, Germany, and the Ottoman Empire, which had hoped to gain influence in the Persian Gulf in the late 19th and early 20th

Present-day Al-Fujairah, one of the seven trucial states along the Arabian peninsula.

centuries. After World War II (1939–45), however, Great Britain declined as a world power and began to lose its colonial holdings, including India in 1947. In 1951 and 1952 the British helped establish a Trucial defense force and a council to discuss common problems faced by these states.

In 1968 Great Britain announced that it would remove its military forces from the Gulf region by the end of 1971. During these same years oil discoveries by Western oil companies were just beginning to modernize Abu Dhabi. Although the ruling family of Abu Dhabi was not prepared for the loss of British defensive support or the beginnings of great oil wealth, the sheikh was eager to create regional unity.

First, following the British announcement, Abu Dhabi and Dubai agreed to form a federation. Then, in 1970 Shayk Zayid ibn Sultan al-Nahyan, the ruler of Abu Dhabi, made the bold announcement that the oil revenues were to be "at the service of all the emirates." The Trucial States—Sharjah, 'Ajman, Umm al-Qaywayn, Ra's al-Khaymah, and al-Fujayrah—were invited to join Abu Dhabi and Dubai in the federation, as were Qatar and Bahrain.

In each emirate a strong desire for security was tempered by an equally strong desire to maintain tribal independence. While Bahrain and Qatar declined to join, six of the emirates agreed on a federation in December 1971, with Ra's al-Khaymah holding out for two months before signing on in February 1972.

The rulers of the emirates knew that the oil discoveries made it essential for them to unite for security reasons, and world events soon confirmed their reasoning. The ambitions of the communist Soviet Union and its invasion of Afghanistan were one cause for alarm. The Iran-Iraq War, which began in 1980, and the continuing Arab-Israeli conflict also revealed how volatile the region was and is. In addition, Iran occupied two Gulf islands claimed by Sharjah and Ra's al-Khaymah, a dispute that has not yet been resolved. Iraq's invasion of Kuwait in 1990 brought the danger very close to home.

These events have made it clear that the UAE and its neighboring oil-producing countries are of tremendous importance to the world. To aid in their own defense, the UAE in 1981 joined with the five other oil-rich monarchies—Saudi Arabia, Kuwait, Bahrain, Qatar, and Oman—to form the Gulf Cooperation Council. They also rely on the major nations that depend on their oil, especially the United States for protection against other countries that threaten their sovereignty. The United States, in turn,

UAE troops being inspected. Even though it has its own defense force, the UAE continues to rely on countries like the United States for protection.

Since the oil boom in the UAE, oil wells like this have become a familiar sight.

showed its commitment to the Gulf states' independence in 1990, when it rushed to the aid of Kuwait after Iraq, led by the dictator Saddam Hussein, invaded.

THE UAE OIL BOOM

Most of the Gulf monarchies had signed agreements with consortiums, or combinations of Western oil companies, beginning in the 1930s. In 1959, following earlier discoveries of oil in Saudi Arabia and Kuwait, oil was found in Abu Dhabi. More discoveries followed, but Dubai had to wait another ten years for its own oil to start flowing. When the offshore and land discoveries were surveyed, experts found that the UAE was perched atop about 98 billion barrels of oil, constituting about 10 percent of the world's total. Most of the oil is in Abu Dhabi, with Dubai a distant second. The other emirates have little or no oil. In the 1970s the UAE became one of the original members of the Organization of the Petroleum and Exporting Countries (OPEC).

Over the next three decades the UAE was transformed. Poverty and hunger disappeared; and shabby streets and houses were replaced by spectacular high-rise luxury hotels, office buildings, and apartment complexes. The Emirati and their leaders have since settled into intelligent, farsighted planning of the federation's future.

The UAE has adopted a moderate stand in its dealings with other oil-producing countries and with the world, and it has become a supporter of the United States-led war on terrorism. Following the terrorist attacks on the United States on September 11, 2001, it was found that some of the funds used by the terrorists had been funneled through UAE banks. The UAE

Storage tanks at an UAE oil refinery.

government cracked down instantly, closing accounts and freezing the assets of anyone suspected of involvement. Since then the federation has worked closely with U.S. and international agencies against terroism.

Since the 1980s the people of the seven emirates and their rulers have been involved in the rapid transformation of their country. They are trying to adjust to modern lifestyles, while also trying to retain and even expand their traditional arts and crafts. They are also seeking ways to protect the desert and coastal environment. Another thorny issue involves finding ways to incorporate hundreds of thousands of newcomers from other parts of the world into UAE society without destroying their traditional Arab customs and values. The UAE's oil bonanza, and its new importance to the world, makes it clear that the future will not be anything like the country's poverty-stricken and rather isolated past.

GOVERNMENT

WHEN ABU DHABI AND DUBAI announced the formation of a federation in 1971, many outside observers were skeptical as it had never been done in modern times. But the United Arab Emirates defied the experts. The federation of seven emirates, completed in February 1972, has lasted for more than 30 years, even though there are huge differences in population, wealth, and importance among the individual emirates. Another reason behind initial skepticism was that the rulers had no experience in operating a federal government. Before 1972, when the emirates were known as the Trucial States, there had been no national government, and the British had managed their foreign affairs and defense.

The guiding force in the creation of the UAE was the ruler of Abu Dhabi, Shayk Zayid ibn Sultan al-Nahyan. The resulting government is unique among federal governments and involves a delicate balancing act between the national government and the seven emirates. The rulers of the smaller emirates have to protect their family and tribal interests while also working for the good of the country. The rulers of Abu Dhabi and Dubai have to be careful not to dominate, even though they could exercise overwhelming power. They could cause resentment, for example, by insisting that oil revenues be used only as they wished.

THE FEDERAL GOVERNMENT: BALANCING LOYALTIES

The Emirati are proud of their young nation, but they also feel deep loyalty toward their families, their tribes, and to the sheikh of their emirate. The importance of these loyalties is evident in many aspects of the government. According to the 1971 constitution, for example, the president and vice president are to be elected every five years by the Supreme Council. In

Opposite: **The municipal building in Dubai.**

practice, however, the president is always a member of the al-Nahyan clan of Abu Dhabi, and the vice president and premier are from Dubai's al-Maktoum tribe.

Shayk Zayid ibn Sultan al-Nahyan was the UAE's first president, serving from its founding in 1972 until his death on November 2, 2004. His son, Khalifa ibn Zayid al-Nahyan, was elected to replace him the next day. Similarly, Vice President Sheikh Mohammed bin Rashid al-Maktoum was elected by the Supreme Council in January 2006 to replace his brother.

The Federal Supreme Council of Rulers is made up of the rulers of all seven emirates. In addition to electing the president and vice president, the Council acts as the highest constitutional authority, setting general policies for the country. The seven rulers meet four times a year and decisions are made by consensus. That is, all seven members of the

UAE President Shayk Khalifa ibn Zayid al-Nahyan addresses the 26th Gulf Cooperation Council Summit in Abu Dhabi in 2005.

SHAYK ZAYID IBN SULTAN AL-NAHYAN: FATHER OF THE UAE

Shayk Zayid ibn Sultan al-Nahyan (1918–2004) was far more than the first president of the UAE. He was the driving force behind the creation of the federation, possessing the vision, strength, and skill needed to bring unity to seven desert emirates. He served as president from 1972 until his death in 2004.

Born in 1918 in al-'Ayn, he always felt deep affection for the oasis. The famous British explorer Wilfred Thesiger met him in the 1940s and described him in *Arabian Sands* as "a powerfully built man...with a brown beard. He had a strong, intelligent face...and his manner was quite masterful. . . . He wore a dagger and cartridge belt; his rifle lay on the sand beside him.

He had a great reputation among the Bedu. They liked him for his easy, informal ways and his friendliness, and they respected his force of character."

Shayk Zayid spent many of his early days moving stones and planting trees to restore the ancient system of canals needed to irrigate the date palms of his beloved al-'Ayn. In 1966 he replaced his brother Shakhbut, who had ruled Abu Dhabi since 1928.

In working to create the federation after the British announced their withdrawal from the Persian Gulf, his Highness showed great skill in establishing harmony among the seven very different emirates. He built their confidence in Abu Dhabi and the federation by helping the poorer emirates financially and creating huge public works programs throughout the country.

One of Shayk Zayid's special projects was "greening the desert" by using desalinated water for landscaping and planting. The city of Abu Dhabi now boasts 24 parks and 3,700 acres (1,500 ha) of grass, watered by electric sprinklers and decorated with splendid fountains. Making the desert bloom seems a fitting tribute to the father of the UAE.

Shayk Mohammed ibn Rashid al-Maktoum, vice president and prime minister of the UAE, casts his vote at a polling station in Dubai in December 2006.

Supreme Council must be in agreement for a policy to be established. In practice the rulers of Abu Dhabi and Dubai can veto any measure they disapprove of, but both rulers try to avoid this, and they work hard to achieve a consensus on every issue.

FEDERAL STRUCTURE AND FUNCTIONS

When the federation was formed in 1971, the seven rulers agreed to turn certain functions over to the federal government. In general the Supreme Council of Rulers, headed by the president and vice president, is responsible for the foreign affairs, security and defense, public health, education, currency, matters of nationality and immigration, and postal and telecommunications of the country. Other functions of the federal government include air-traffic control, labor relations, issues involving territorial waters, and the extradition of criminals. All other domestic matters are left to the individual emirates.

THE EXECUTIVE BRANCH The main executive body for carrying out these federal functions is the Council of Ministers, which operates much like a cabinet does in other countries. The Council of Ministers consists of various department heads, such as the minister of labor and the minister of education. The ministers are headed by a prime minister, appointed by the president and the Supreme Council of Rulers.

All the other ministers are similarly chosen, and they can come from any of the emirates. To ensure that the interests of all the emirates are represented, efforts are made to select at least one or two ministers from every emirate.

THE LEGISLATIVE BRANCH The UAE version of a parliament is called the Federal National Council (FNC), and is not to be confused with the Supreme Council of Rulers or the Council of Ministers. This is a one-house body made up of 40 members chosen for two-year terms by the rulers of the emirates. In the 2006 elections half the seats were appointed as before and half by councils in each emirate.

The 40 members are chosen by a fixed ratio, according to population. Currently, the FNC has eight members each from Abu Dhabi and Dubai, six each from Sharjah and Ra's al-Khaymah, and four each from al-Fujayrah, Umm al-Qaywayn, and 'Ajman.

The main function of the FNC is not to create or propose legislation, as legislative bodies do in other countries. Instead, the 40 members "review" new measures passed by the Supreme Council of Rulers. They can suggest changes but not actually make them.

The existence of the FNC gives people and ruling families in the smaller emirates a real sense of participation. The Arab name for FNC is Majlis Watani Ittihad. The word majlis refers to an ancient custom in which anyone can appear before a ruler to state needs, suggestions, opinions, or complaints. This has always enabled people to feel that they are involved in the government and for the ruler to hear what might be troubling his subjects.

THE JUDICIARY The constitution establishes an independent judiciary for national matters. The judges for this Union Supreme Court are appointed by the president.

LOCAL GOVERNMENTS When the federation was formed, all seven emirates had long-established governments. All were, and are, controlled by the ruling family and its sheikh, or emir. The sheikhs hold regular majlis within their own emirates, as they have done for many years.

The Abu Dhabi government is the largest and most complex. Called the National Consultative Council, it is made up of members of the oldest families and tribes in the emirate.

The main cities also have Municipal Councils. These urban councils manage such matters as traffic control, minor crimes, and sanitation.

TROUBLESOME ISSUES

Because of the loyalty of people to their families, tribes, and shayk, the boundaries between emirates were rather loosely drawn. Families that technically belonged to one emirate might actually belong to a tribe in a neighboring emirate. The result is the existence of small enclaves of people who feel that they do not belong to the emirate in which they are physically located. About 10 miles (16 km) inside the border of Abu Dhabi, for example, there are small settlements of people who belong to al-Fujayrah's Sharqiyyin tribal group.

Similarly, the UAE's boundaries with Saudi Arabia and Oman have never been permanently drawn. Treaties have been signed in the past three or four years, but the provisions have not been made public, so it is not clear exactly what agreements have been made.

A second problem is related to international drug trafficking. Because of the UAE's geographic position between the drug-producing regions of Southern Asia and drug buyers in Europe and the Middle East, it has become subject to money laundering by large banking and investment companies. The country's antimoney-laundering laws and policing techniques have improved steadily since 2000.

Members of the Emirati delegation attend a counter-terror conference in Riyadh, Saudi Arabia, in 2005.

TERRORISM AND THE UAE

After the September 11, 2001, terrorist attacks on New York and Washington, DC, and the plane crash in Pennsylvania, the United States launched its war against terrorists throughout the world. Antiterrorism agents soon discovered that two of the eleven highjackers were citizens of the UAE. They also found that some of the funds used by the terrorists had come from bank accounts in Dubai.

UAE officials worked closely with American agents to close the bank accounts and to tighten the laws governing banks in the emirates. They also supplied information about any individuals in the UAE suspected of having ties to terrorist organizations. In addition, the emirates continued to make their port and airfield facilities available to U.S. military forces. These efforts convinced most U.S. leaders that the emirates were genuine allies. Early in 2006 the U.S. State Department reported that the UAE has been "a solid and cooperative partner in the fight against terrorism."

A CONFLICT OVER U.S. PORTS

Early in 2006 a government-owned company—Dubai Ports World, or "DP World"—announced that it had purchased a British shipping company for $6.8 billion. The deal created a sudden furor when the American press and politicians learned that the deal involved DP World taking control of six American ports, including the ports of New York (*below*) and New Jersey. Although the arrangement had quietly been approved by the Bush administration and its security agencies, critics charged that it placed American ports at the mercy of a country that had been tied to the 9/11 attacks.

Administration officials and the director of DP World tried to assure the skeptics that the UAE was a firm ally and that there was no danger to U.S. ports. Supporters of the deal also pointed out that, of the roughly 2 billion tons of cargo handled by U.S. ports each year, only about 5 percent of the cargo containers entering the United States are ever examined. The critics, especially in the U.S. Senate, continued to insist that the arrangement be reexamined. Instead, the directors of DP World decided to avoid further controversy by withdrawing their offer to manage the American port facilities. As soon as that announcement was made, the uproar quickly subsided.

ECONOMY

FIRST-TIME VISITORS TO THE great cities of the United Arab Emirates—Dubai, Abu Dhabi, and Sharjah—run out of superlatives in their efforts to describe the wonders: sparkling new office and apartment towers; ultraluxurious resort hotels (including the world's only seven-star hotel); beautiful tree-lined avenues decorated with parks and fountains; and unbelievable shopping malls, some with more than 500 shops. Out in the water, there are even more spectacles such as Palm Island, which consists of seventeen gracefully shaped "palm fronds" made of sand dredged from far out in the Indian Ocean. The artificial island, already receiving occupants, will be home to more than 120,000 people residing in luxury homes. The world's tallest building, when completed in 2008, will be the Burj Dubai (*burj* is Arabic for tower), rising more than 2,600 feet (792 m). Three more islands shaped like palm trees are well under way, as is a set of islands arranged in the shape of the world.

Above: **The Burj Al Arab Hotel in Dubai, viewed from across Jumeirah Beach, is a 7-star hotel.**

Opposite: **Many Emrati still depend on small-scale trading such as selling fish to support themselves and their families.**

Some of the developments can appear outlandish, such as constructing the world's largest aquarium and the world's largest amusement park. In fact, however, the huge building boom is part of a farsighted plan to turn the UAE into one of the world's greatest tourist destinations. Tourism is one of the key industries the UAE is developing in order to diversify its economy. The people and their rulers are determined to build a future that does not depend solely on oil.

Camels are still used as a mode of transport, as seen here on a street in Dubai.

THE TRADITIONAL ECONOMY

Before the oil boom, the people of today's UAE were all too familiar with poverty and hunger. A survey of the pre-oil economy provides the background needed to understand how the people and the government are using their new-found wealth.

AGRICULTURE Arab families in the coastal areas, mountain wadis, and oases relied on irrigation and wells to grow their date palms and crops. The date palm was their all encompassing plant, used to make houses, tents, farming tools, fishing nets, and small boats.

The scarcity of water made camels the most important livestock. They were used primarily for transportation and were known as the ships of the desert. The animals could go without water for up to two weeks in the summer, and two or three months in the winter. The camels were also a source of milk, meat, and wool. The fertile land around the oases, coasts, and mountain also supported goats and sheep, which were important sources of wool, meat, and milk.

Farm life was hard, but the life of the desert Bedu tribe was far harder. The Bedu engaged in a continual search for grazing land and water for their flocks and camels. Thirst and starvation were constant dangers.

LIFE FROM THE SEA Family and tribal ties formed a web that linked the people of the inland oases to the people of the coast. Often, the men would move to the coast in the spring to spend the summer diving for pearls.

Coastal people relied on small-scale trading, pearl diving, and fishing to survive. They used an amazing array of dhows, whose sizes, shapes, and construction were determined by their intended use. Different designs were used for fishing, pearl diving, and long-distance trade; smaller boats were used for transportation on the creeks.

Fishing provided not only food but, for families owning a boat, a source of revenue. The warm waters of the Persian Gulf support more than 700 species of fish. Usually, men went to sea to fish, and women sold the catch. Fish were caught in nets or in cleverly designed cages known as *gargour*, which were made of palm leaves. Some of the fish were dried and stored or exported.

THE EARLY COPPER TRADE

Today the UAE's oil is exported to other countries. Centuries ago another underground resource, copper, was mined and shipped to other places. Archaeological sites in the UAE and Oman show that the people of the region were mining, processing, and exporting copper as early as 3000 B.C. It is estimated that over several centuries more than 4,000 tons of copper were exported. The copper trade apparently continued through the Middle Ages.

In an effort to reduce the UAE's dependence on oil revenues, copper mining has been reintroduced on a small scale. An added bonus of refining the copper has been the discovery of small pockets of gold and silver.

Fishermen catch sardines in Khor Kalba, Sharjah.

Pearling was a good part-time occupation, at least until the 1930s, and it also promised divers the possibility of fabulous wealth. However, it was a dangerous life. Wearing nose clips made of turtle shells, the men dived to 98 feet (30 m) or more and stayed submerged for up to three minutes.

The coastal towns also were the centers of the maritime trade. Even before the oil boom began, for example, Dubai had been promoting trade between India and markets in the Middle East and Europe. In addition, market areas, called souks were found in these towns, which were divided into separate quarters according to the trade involved. Some sold food, while others specialized in spices or in handicrafts, such as pottery, wooden items, or jewelry.

THE OIL BONANZA

The first discovery of oil was made in Abu Dhabi in 1959, and the first exports began three years later. The discovery of oil in Dubai came a little later, with exports beginning in 1969. Today the UAE is known to have 98 billion barrels of oil, 10 percent of the world's total. Abu Dhabi owns the lion's share of that treasure—92 billion barrels, enough to last well past the end of the century. Dubai, with 4 billion barrels (about 30 years' worth at current production rates) has the only other meaningful supply. Sharjah and Ra's al-Khaymah have small pockets of a light grade of crude oil called condensate, but it is not enough to support a major industry.

Sharjah, however, also has natural gas, part of the country's reserves of 210.43 trillion cubic feet (6.3 trillion cubic meter), one of the largest supplies in the world. The development of the new industry of exporting liquefied natural gas (LNG) is now under way.

Workers walking along pipes that connect to oil storage tanks at the Jebel Ali Port.

The oil boom was given a terrific boost by changes in the world market. The UAE was one of the first of the thirteen countries to join OPEC. In 1973 OPEC quadrupled the price of oil then made another huge increase in 1979. In 1979 the price of a barrel of crude oil leaped from about $5 to $34.

The UAE was suddenly awash, not in oil but in oil money along with three other Gulf states: Saudi Arabia, Kuwait, and Qatar. They, when combined with the UAE, held 45 percent of the world's oil. At first, both the people and their leaders were giddy with oil riches. European and American businesspeople rushed to the Persian Gulf to propose all sorts of construction and investment schemes.

Abu Dhabi's emir and the president of the federation, Shayk Zayid, kept his pledge to help the poorer emirates. Major programs were launched in each of the emirates to develop infrastructure: electric power, roads, airports, harbor facilities, schools, hospitals, and clinics.

DEVELOPING A MODERN ECONOMY

By the late 1980s the UAE had nearly completed its infrastructure. The rulers had also created the ideal welfare state. There were no taxes; and every Emirati was guaranteed an education and employment. Medical care was provided for free in luxurious, well-equipped hospitals. Utilities, such as water, electricity, and oil products, were almost free.

The rulers, and the planners they hired, worked to find ways to diversify the economy so as to become less dependent on oil. Desalination plants were built to provide water for the cities and to expand green areas. Local agriculture was promoted, resulting in a remarkable increase in agricultural output to the extent that today, Dubai is able to export strawberries to Europe during the winter months.

Other plans included developing industries, including a state-of-the-art aluminum plant. Steel, petrochemical, and concrete plants soon followed. More recently, companies and factories have been created for food processing, furniture production, and pharmaceuticals production.

Another major move was the establishment of the Jebel Ali Free Zone created by the Dubai government in 1985. In this huge area covering 38 square miles (100 square km), Dubai provides tax-free shipping and storage facilities with the world's largest artificial port, including ready-made factories and living quarters for workers. Transportation and communications systems are up to date. In other words, a company can simply sign a lease for all the buildings and other facilities it needs and commence its manufacturing operation. Black & Decker, Heinz, Honda, Reebok, and Sony are among the 800 companies manufacturing at Jebel Ali.

One of the most exciting and visible areas of growth has been the tourism industry. The UAE's three main cities have outstanding facilities for tourists, such as several five-star hotels and restaurants, beaches and swimming pools, amusement parks, and museums. Vacationers can take trips from the cities into the desert or to oases. There are also horse races, golf courses, dhow excursions, fishing, and dolphin watches. Perhaps one of the most surprising aspects of the UAE's tourism industry is the number of wealthy people from other countries who have purchased vacation homes there.

The Palm and The World islands have attracted property buyers from all over the world.

Expatriate workers in the fish souk cleaning station in Sharjah.

EXPATRIATE WORKERS

UAE rulers and business leaders are eager to employ Emirati in executive positions, but the lack of qualified professionals has made that difficult. Consequently, foreign workers have been hired to fill a wide variety of jobs, from simple construction tasks to marine zoology research.

Many of the foreign workers, or expatriates, receive excellent salaries and company benefits, and that proves to be a strong enough incentive for them to leave home for months or years at a time. To attract qualified workers, some companies offer special incentives, such as paid leave once or twice a year, and sometimes a round-trip airline ticket.

There are negative aspects of being an expatriate worker. In almost all cases, for example, expatriates cannot become UAE citizens. They do not enjoy many of the benefits of citizenship, such as getting free education, health care, electricity, and water. More serious are the

allegations that some workers are being mistreated by being forced to
work long hours, for example, or to work under hazardous or unhealthy
conditions. In addition, reports indicate that workers from Southern and
Southeastern Asia work mostly in menial jobs, such as driving taxis and
performing unskilled work in the petroleum industry. Many are forced
into these jobs when they lose their better jobs to Emirati who have
completed training.

In spite of the difficulties many expatriates remain either because they
enjoy the life or they cannot resist the wages, even though salaries have
declined a little in the past few years. Some also go to the UAE to escape
unrest in their home countries, such as Lebanon and Palestine. Expatriates
continue to make up about 75 percent of the UAE's population.

Some expatriates have lived in the UAE since the oil boom days of
the 1970s. Their children have grown up in the UAE and have gone to
local schools. The result is a mixing of ethnicities and cultures, which
enriches life in the UAE. Some Emirati are concerned, however, because
they are a minority in their own country. They worry that their traditional
values and customs may disappear.

The headquaters of Daim-lerChrysler in Michigan. The UAE has reduced its input into new economic projects and invested billions in companies like DaimlerChrysler.

PLANNING UAE'S FUTURE

In the 1980s there was a glut of oil on the world market, and the prices of petroleum products dropped sharply. This jolted the economy of the UAE, as well as other oil-rich Gulf countries. The UAE found itself, like other countries of the world, building up a sizable national debt. The rulers became determined to plan more wisely in the future.

The world market soon bounced back, and oil prices returned to $34 a barrel. The market was shaken in a different way in 2005 when oil shortages developed, and by the close of the year, prices had shot to almost $70 a barrel, doubling revenues for the OPEC countries.

Instead of pouring some 80 percent of the revenues into new projects, as in the past, the UAE now uses only about 40 percent to foster economic expansion. Much of the wealth is now used to reduce its debt and to invest in safe stock and bond markets. In 2005, for example, the UAE purchased $1 billion in shares of the auto manufacturer DaimlerChrysler. Even greater amounts were invested in U.S. Treasury bonds, which help to finance America's huge debt.

The wise and cautious planning has not stopped architects and designers from coming up with fantastic construction schemes, but the planners are clearly creating a future that will be less dependent on oil. Economists estimate that oil revenues now account for only about 30 percent of the UAE's income, or gross domestic product. In addition, the country's moderate foreign policy has allowed it to play an important role in the affairs of the region. Its friendly attitude toward Europe and the United States has also helped to boost its fast-growing tourism industry.

DUTY-FREE DUBAI

Tourists flock to the UAE, especially Dubai, to purchase tax-free luxuries. This form of tourism has been carefully cultivated. In order to attract airplanes to stop over in Dubai on their way from Europe to the Far East and Australia, the UAE created tax-free outlets at international airports. Dubai has become one of the most popular tax-free shopping centers in the world. Businesspeople and tourists find it worth their while to route their journeys through Dubai. Abu Dhabi has now approached Dubai's reputation for offering myriad tax-free items.

For those bringing goods into the country, Dubai's tax-free limits are the most generous in the world. Tax-free does not only mean that there is a wide array of shops at the international airports. The UAE is a tax-free country, so there is no income tax, purchase tax, or value-added tax, as there is in other countries. Shoppers have been known to travel all the way from Europe to purchase anything from caviar to cars.

The tax-free or duty-free concept has been helped by generations of trading traditions in the Gulf. With competition between Abu Dhabi and Dubai, tourists can only benefit.

ENVIRONMENT

DESERT ENVIRONMENTS CONTAIN remarkably fragile ecosystems. Damage to one part of the system, such as the drying up of an underground spring, reverberates throughout the entire system. Some plant and animal species can die out or animals can move away, creating further changes in the system.

In general, the Emirati have lived in harmony with their environment. A desert culture tries not to put pressure on the land and works within the limits of the ecosystem. Traditional farmers, for example, would make only modest changes to the environment by extending their stone-lined irrigation channels.

Above: **Heavy traffic in Dubai has resulted in a higher level of air pollution in the city.**

Opposite: **A tourist peers over the sides of the Hatta rock pools found near the ancient village of Hatta in Dubai.**

The oil boom changed the human-environment equation. Money gave the United Arab Emirates access to modern technology, and the ability to make radical changes to the environment. Many of the changes have made the desert a much more comfortable place to live in. The ambitious use of desalinated water has given the country the power to "make the desert bloom." The extensive use of air-conditioning in homes, motor vehicles, and public buildings has certainly made it easier to live in temperatures that frequently reach 110°F (43°C).

As all modern societies have learned, the power to change the environment can also lead to unintended negative consequences. The leaders of the UAE have shown unusual awareness of the awesome power the oil wealth has given them, and they are using it to take steps to reduce the harmful environmental effects of their activities.

Dubai Zoo officials with lion cubs, live falcons, stuffed nile crocodiles, and animal skins, including those of the rare snow leopard, seized at Dubai Airport in 2003.

ENDANGERED SPECIES

Long before the drilling of oil, hunting reduced the populations of many desert mammals. Some were hunted for food by the Bedu and others were hunted as trophies by large hunting parties organized by wealthy sheikhs. The populations of some predators, such as the Arabian leopard, have also been reduced, because they posed a danger to livestock.

In addition to the Arabian leopard, other endangered species include the Arabian tahr, a goatlike animal that lives high in the mountains. The tahr was thought to be extinct, but a 1995 wildlife survey found that some survive at altitudes above 2,000 feet (600 m). The survival of the Arabian gazelle was also discovered during the same 1995 survey. The lynx caracal, a reddish brown, nocturnal cat, seems to have survived by hunting at night and sleeping during the day. Several other mammals, including the desert wolf, Gordon's wildcat, and the striped hyena, are rarely seen in the wild.

Several ruling families have been active in protecting these and other rare species. The late president Shayk Zayid ibn Sultan al-Nahyan was one of the pioneers of the country's ambitious conservation efforts. He transformed an island off the coast of Abu Dhabi into the Sir Bani Yas Nature Reserve. Endangered species roam the island freely, and there is hope that some populations might become large enough to return a few to the wild.

The Arabian Leopard Trust has been very active in creating public education campaigns in the hopes of saving a number of endangered species in addition to the Arabian leopard. It was this group that conducted the 1995 survey that provided an important census of the UAE's wildlife.

THE ARABIAN LEOPARD

Perhaps the best known of the desert species, the Arabian leopard is found only in the al-Hajar Mountains of the UAE, bordering Oman. These leopards, known in the UAE as panthers, are also found in a few other remote areas of the Arabian Peninsula. While somewhat smaller than other leopards, they are magnificent and powerful cats, with some males reaching a length of 4 to 6 feet (2 to 3 m) and a weight of 65 to 70 pounds (29 to 32 kg).

The Arabian Leopard Trust (ALT) estimates that only about 100 of these cats still exist throughout the entire Arabian Peninsula, and perhaps as few as 20 live in the al-Hajar Mountains. In addition to its education campaign, the ALT also conducts research and works with rescued leopards in the hope of raising cubs that can eventually be released into the wild.

ENVIRONMENTAL DANGERS

In the late 1990s a construction company's fleet sailed into the Indian Ocean to dredge hundreds of tons of sand from the ocean floor. The ships returned to the UAE and dumped the sand in carefully mapped locations. Gradually the Palm Islands, the narrow, gracefully curved islands bolstered by thousands of boulders, took shape.

By late 2005 the Palm Islands were nearly complete. Its streets are lined with stylish homes, all of which were sold before completion, mostly to wealthy people from other parts of the world. Paved streets and trees covered underground electricity, water, and sewer lines.

Environmentalists have an array of questions about this ambitious project. Will erosion wear away these artificial islands? Does their proximity to the shore significantly alter the action of waves and tides along the coast? Will the region's marine life be disrupted by the huge construction

Contractors constructing the Palm Islands know precisely where to spray each load of sand by using a Global Positioning System.

project? Along with the rapid growth of the entire city of Dubai, can the coastal ecosystem support so many people?

The UAE developers seem unconcerned, because they say they have analyzed most of the potential problems. In some cases the problems have been minimal. Marine life seems to be thriving around the new islands, for example, and fragile coral reefs have actually expanded enough to create a new area for snorkeling. Another potential problem, the flow of coastal waters, seems to have been resolved by cutting strategically located openings in the causeway connecting the islands to the mainland.

The rulers of the UAE realize that not all potential problems have been addressed or even identified. Every project is still carefully monitored for its environmental impact. In addition, the country has engaged in a variety of environmental conservation and protection programs, often involving international experts and organizations. However, environmental concerns will undoubtedly continue as the UAE builds more artificial islands.

The UAE has become a party to many international agreements on the environment, including Biodiversity; Climate Change; Climate Change— Kyoto Protocol; Desertification; Endangered Species; Marine Dumping Treaty; and Ozone Layer Protection. The Law of the Sea was recently signed but is not yet ratified.

One of the Palm Islands taking shape.

In May 1999, Abu Dhabi completed the al-Khazna groundwater project, which provides 50 million gallons of groundwater per day, substantially reducing the emirate's dependence on desalinated water.

SPECIAL ENVIRONMENTAL PROGRAMS

The careful management of water resources is a matter of vital importance to desert nations. In the UAE, for example, experts in water management have found that, even with the ambitious desalination programs currently in place, the country faces serious water issues. One problem involves the oases and other agricultural regions, where the overuse of irrigation has led to a buildup of salt in the soil, resulting in a sharp decline in agricultural productivity.

To address these and other water issues, the UAE government invited local, regional, and international environmentalists, scientists, and agriculture experts to attend a seminar in February 2006. The seminar, Sustainable Environment and Water Resources (EWR2006), made a series of recommendations for firm regulations on the use of groundwater in farming areas. The experts also suggested the use of a system called solar distillation as the simplest and most efficient method of desalination. A third recommendation was that the huge amounts of water produced during oil production be used to water crops. But, they warned, more study is needed to determine how this water could be cleaned and to make sure that the use of the water would not be harmful to humans or the environment.

Another illustration of the UAE's commitment to environmental protection and conservation is the series of annual international conferences it holds on the date palm. The third conference, held in February 2006, involved more than 150 participants from 35 countries, including the United States. Their conference sought to find environmentally safe ways to increase production and ways to deal with pests, such as the red palm weevil, which threatens date palms in several countries.

In early 2006 Abu Dhabi hosted conferences on nutrition education, diabetes research, the geology of the Middle East, and the state of the Gulf ecosystem.

"GREENING" THE DESERT

The late president, Shayk Zayid, was devoted to the dream of "greening" the desert, and he made use of Abu Dhabi's oil revenues to advance that dream. The use of desalinated water from the Gulf made the project feasible. All citizens of the UAE are encouraged to participate, and any homeowner can get trees and outdoor plants at no cost.

The president's program led to the creation of more than 20 parks in Abu Dhabi City and some 3,700 acres (1,500 ha) of grass. At his beloved oasis, al-'Ayn, there are close to 40 parks, many with pools or fountains. The added greenery has helped to ease the oppressive summer heat and has made the cities more pleasant for visitors. An unexpected benefit has been an increase in birdlife.

EMIRATI

THE POPULATION OF THE UNITED Arab Emirates is growing fast, and it is remarkably diverse. Demographers estimate that the population was about 180,000 when the federation was formed in 1971, 35 years later it has grown to more than 2,500,000. Arab nationals numbered barely one out of every five people. In spite of the rapid change and growth, visitors are struck by the friendliness of the people and the absence of serious tension between the various ethnic groups.

Two customs, developed over many centuries, help to explain this openness and tolerance. First, in desert Arab cultures hospitality is a basic rule of survival. A Bedu herdsman, miles from any oasis, on seeing strangers approach, will automatically start preparing coffee and rush out to greet them. This custom of hospitality is still important in modern life. Although today's city dwellers are more reserved, they are still willing to drop everything to help someone in need.

The second custom, openness to people from other cultures, emerges from the long history of seafaring and coastal trade in the region. This has helped to make coastal people in the UAE open to new ideas and new people.

Keeping these two customs in balance is a shrewd business sense. The merchants and businesspeople of the UAE have a reputation for being tough bargainers. Whether in an elegant steel and glass business tower or in a rug merchant's souk, they will haggle over prices until they are satisfied that the deal is fair.

Above: **Bedouins set up camp in the desert. They are known for their generous hospitality.**

Opposite: **Emrati men taking a walk along the docks in Dubai.**

A group of Emirati men relaxing in Dubai.

The largest city in the UAE is Dubai City, which contains about 90 percent of the emirate's 750,000 people. The nation's capital, Abu Dhabi City, has about 540,000 people.

THE ETHNIC MIX

Out of a population estimated at 2,602,713 in 2006, roughly 1 million, or about 40 percent, live in the emirate of Abu Dhabi. The next largest population centers are Dubai, with about 750,000, and Sharjah, with 636,000. The other emirates have populations the size of those in many American towns; Ajman has about 275,000, Ra's al-Kaymah 230,000, al-Fujayrah has 130,000, and Umm al-Qaywayn has 75,000.

Only about 20 percent of the people are UAE nationals. The rest are expatriates from all parts of the world, drawn to the emirates primarily by job and business opportunities.

Other Arabs and Iranians account for 23 percent of the nation's non-national population. People from Southern Asian countries—such as India, Pakistan, the Philippines, and Bangladesh—make up roughly 50 percent of the non-national population. The remaining 8 percent consists of Europeans, Americans, and Eastern Asians (Japanese and Chinese).

A major difference in the appearance of the UAE's population is that so many are dressed in the Arab or Muslim loose-fitting white robe. Different-colored headdresses often indicate an individual's country of origin or tribal allegiance. UAE Arabs wear a white headdress held on by a double-twisted black thong, while Saudis wear a checkered headdress, and Syrians wear one with red and white checks.

INEQUALITY

Although there are no visible signs of ethnic tension, many human rights groups are concerned about the treatment of expatriate workers, especially the great numbers from Asian countries. These organizations report that wages are based on nationality rather than on job qualifications. There are also reports of discrimination against women and older workers.

While the official population estimate is 2,602,713 some international agencies say the number is considerably higher because of the great numbers of foreign workers.

Women in traditional burkhas. Many human rights groups are concerned over the alleged discrimination against female workers in the UAE.

65

Some international agencies, as well as the U.S. government, are urging the UAE to sign the major conventions of the International Labor Organization. This would allow the formation of unions and permit strikes, both of which are currently banned in the UAE. The government in Abu Dhabi responds that no one is being forced to work in the emirates and that non-nationals are there to take advantage of the high wages and the high standard of living.

DESERT CONNECTIONS

Although the UAE is a new nation, the shared heritage of the people has helped to bind them into a single identity. Islam and the Arab identity of the people are part of that heritage and so is their connection to the desert.

Arab tribes moved into the deserts of today's UAE more than 2,500 years ago. Most settled into permanent communities, some in coastal towns, and others in the oases and other inland fertile areas, where they lived by farming and raising some livestock. Somewhat smaller numbers were the Bedu, "dwellers of the desert" in Arabic, who maintained their nomadic lifestyle, permanently engaged in a hard struggle for survival.

Today most UAE nationals live in coastal cities and towns. Through family and tribal ties, however, urbanized families maintain close connections with those living inland, including the Bedu. Many Arabs feel a sense of identity with the Bedu. They maintain a romanticized image of the rugged and independent nomads in a way that is not unlike Americans' feelings for the heroes of the "Wild West," including Native Americans. Over hundreds of years stories of the desert culture was handed down orally, and the Bedu became the heroes of many stories, poems, and songs.

An Emirati with his herd of camels in the desert of Abu Dhabi.

THE BEDU INFLUENCE

In the uncertain life of the desert, the concept of hospitality became very complex. When a guest was welcomed to a Bedu tent, for example, he was guaranteed food, shelter, and protection for three and one-third days. This was part of a strict code of honor called *sharaf*. The idea of the three plus days was that, after sharing a meal, the visitor might stay for three days, until all traces of the food had passed through his body. This was known as the bond of salt. If a visitor carried nothing but the host's salt in his system, he would still be under the host's protection.

This code of honor is of great significance to the desert Arab peoples. This honor is upheld by the entire family, and it applies to all aspects of life. The Bedu (and other Arabs) respond that this modesty is a protection of individual and tribal honor.

LIFESTYLE

THE WAY OF LIFE FOR EVERYONE in the United Arab Emirates has been completely transformed by the country's newfound oil wealth. Before the 1970s life was a struggle against grinding poverty and hunger, even starvation. People went barefoot and had no running water or electricity. Health care was almost nonexistent, and women frequently died during childbirth.

But all that has changed. The UAE is now the ultimate modern welfare state. Every citizen is guaranteed an education and a job, or at least an income, if no job is available. There is no income tax and health care is excellent and free. Life expectancy has increased from about 47 years in 1970 to 77 years in 2006.

In spite of the remarkable changes, important elements of the traditional lifestyle remain. The Islamic faith and loyalty to family, clan, and tribe remain the bedrock on which the social structure rests. Other constants, such as honor, friendliness, and generosity continue to be evident in the daily lives of the people.

CITY LIFE

In his book *Arabian Sands*, the English explorer Sir Wilfred Thesiger wrote about his first glimpse of the town of Sharjah in the 1950s, just before the discovery of oil. "We approached a small Arab town on an open beach," he wrote. "It was as drab and tumble-down as Abu Dhabi, but infinitely more squalid, for it was littered with discarded rubbish."

Today, barely 50 years later, Sharjah is a modern city with tree-lined avenues, elegant hotels, and beautiful parks with fountains and ponds. It is also the oldest of the UAE's three major cities (the others being Dubai and Abu Dhabi), and dozens of ancient buildings have been carefully restored, creating a pleasing mixture of the old and the new.

Opposite: **A busy street in the city of Abu Dhabi.**

The seven capital cities of the emirates are all on the coast. Abu Dhabi, the nation's capital, is centered on an island. Dubai, Sharjah, and Ra's al-Khaymah are situated on coastal creeks. 'Ajman, Umm al-Qaywayn, and al-Fujayrah are on sand spits wrapped around lagoons. Roughly 85 percent of the people live in these urban areas, with the majority in Dubai and Abu Dhabi.

The three largest cities are all strikingly modern. Their skylines would not look out of place in Europe or North America, with rows of concrete towers sporting facades of white stone and blue-green glass. To a great extent, Dubai, Abu Dhabi, and Sharjah have been built as magnets for tourists. This is especially true of Dubai, by far the largest and most extravagant city. This is the city with three palm tree shaped islands, along with the archipelago shaped like the world. It is home to the largest

The landscaped lawn of Sheikh Zayid Boulevard in Abu Dhabi, against the neat row of multistory buildings.

aquarium, an indoor ski slope (with real snow), and the 30-square-mile (77 sq km) Dubailand amusement park, which rivals Walt Disney World in size and will soon have the world's tallest building.

Dubai has long been the commercial hub of the country, and the pace of life is faster than that of other cities. There is a very active night life, and alcohol is allowed in many hotels and nightclubs, which is unusual in strict Muslim countries.

Abu Dhabi, the capital, seems somewhat slower paced and perhaps more dignified, possibly because it is the capital. It is also the center of the oil businesses and has many ultramodern office complexes.

Sharjah, located only about 20 minutes from Dubai, is considerably smaller than the other two and has more reminders of its antiquity. There are traditional bazaars and souks, as well as ancient mosques, watchtowers, and forts.

The daily life in all three cities reveals the UAE's ethnic mixing. One might see Iranian rug merchants sharing coffee in a side-street

Children playing at the Ski Dubai Resort at the Mall of the Emirates in Dubai.

souk, while Pakistani women stroll the waterfront, some with baby carriages. As afternoon shadows lengthen, Filipino and Sri Lankan boys gather for a soccer game in a city park, and nearby, Russian tourists snap digital photos in front of a beautiful fountain in Abu Dhabi that spouts water more than 300 feet (122 m) in the air. At an outdoor café, Saudi men discuss a business deal, and several Emirati women prepare for a meeting.

Many people live in high-rise apartment buildings or in modern homes on tree-lined streets on the outskirts of the city. Much of the business takes place in the new office towers, and shoppers head for the elegant, air-conditioned malls, where every brand name in the world can be found, as are shops selling designer originals.

Despite so much that is new, a good deal of business and buying still takes place in the souks, many of them ancient. There, among the flowing, soft colors of Indian silks, people sip strong coffee while haggling over the price of perfumes, carpets, or gold jewelry. The bargaining and the drinking of coffee are integral parts of shopping or closing business deals.

THE COFFEE CEREMONY

Coffee or tea offered to any visitor is a symbol of hospitality. The traditional coffee is called *kahwa* and is made from green coffee beans. It is very strong and can be flavored with cardamom or saffron.

Coffee is served from a traditional pot and poured into small cups without handles. Having three cups of coffee is considered polite, and when the guest has had enough, he or she shakes the cup from side to side to indicate satisfaction.

This social custom of drinking coffee is also important in business. It is a way of cementing relationships, either socially or professionally.

LASTING RURAL TRADITIONS

Although only about 15 percent of the people still live in oases and other rural areas, the rural way of life is imprinted in the minds of the Emirati. Such values as generosity, honor, and hospitality emerged from surviving in a harsh desert environment. Some traditions, however, including those involving the family, are feeling the pressure of the changing modern culture.

For example, women in the UAE have more freedom than those in most Arab Muslim countries. Many women are educated and are free to drive cars, take jobs outside the home, and even operate businesses.

Many marriages are still arranged, although some reports say that this tradition has begun to crumble. Marriage ceremonies continue to be festive affairs, with the two families making the arrangements, including agreement on the gift of money and jewelry given to the bride and her family.

Local women buying gold in Dubai. Women in the UAE are allowed to move around freely and many of them are well educated and are professionals.

Emirati women performing the *ayala*, or hair dance.

On the wedding day the bride's house is decorated with dozens of tiny lights strung from trees and walls. Huge, colorful tents are set up, and tables are crowded with trays of food. The bride traditionally is kept in seclusion for three days prior to the wedding, and she is pampered by family, friends, and a beautician while she wears a traditional green gown and gold jewelry.

Entertainment is a large part of the celebration. This often takes place in a city hotel, with a professional singer and band. Dancing is also important, especially in rural celebrations. Dancing often includes the *ayala*, or hair dance, in which girls swing their long hair as they swirl in circles for hours, accompanied by rhythmic clapping.

Births, which now take place in modern hospitals, are also festive occasions. Visitors bring presents and special foods for the mother. The baby's eyes are lined with a substance called kohl to prevent infection.

TRADITIONAL HOUSING

In the past houses were usually made with wood frames and walls and room dividers made from date palm fronds. Stone houses were built by wealthier families. The traditional *barasti* house had no windows because of the importance of privacy. Instead, each house had a square wind tower, or *badgeer*. Made of stone or palm leaves, the tower was open on four sides to catch any breeze and funnel it into the rooms below.

In a typical *barasti* house, the front room was the public room, and the bedroom was in the rear. Social visits were an important part of daily life and still are. Men and women often socialize separately, with the men in the public part of the house and the women in the family rooms.

The *barasti* house has almost completely disappeared, replaced by modern homes, but many of the traditional social patterns continue with little change. It is still customary to remove one's shoes when entering a house, for example. Food is still an essential element of every visit, with coffee or tea offered as symbols of hospitality. Dates are also frequently served, usually in a preserve called *seh*. When women gather, they may sample perfumes and then burn incense to cleanse the air.

CLOTHING

The traditional dress for women is the aba, also called a *shaili* or *abaya*—a black overgarment and head covering. Under the aba, women wear a loose *sirwal*, or trousers, and a *kandura*—a dress often embroidered in gold or silver. Emerati women also wear a mask covering the nose and mouth called a burka. Many women who originally came from Pakistan, Bangladesh, Sri Lanka, and India wear similar overgarments.

An Emirati woman donning a burka, a mask covering the nose and mouth.

In the Northern Emirates women generally wear brighter, multicolored overgarments.

Men dress in a full-length robe or shirt, called a *dishdash*. The head cloth, or *gutra*, is usually red checked or plain. The black rope wrapped around the head cloth is called the *agal*, and under the headdress they wear a kufi—a small skullcap. Outside the *dishdash* men sometimes wear a cloak, called a *bisht*, which is usually black.

EDUCATION

Before the early 1900s only boys received an education. The traditional school—*al-Katateeb*—offered morning and afternoon sessions on learning to recite passages from the Koran. A new kind of school, still only for boys, was introduced in 1912. These new schools offered training in trade skills and some courses in science. The first schools for girls were opened in 1959.

Education has become very important in the modern nation, for girls as well as for boys. Education is free and compulsory for children ages 6 to 15. Emirati are encouraged to continue their education and earn advanced degrees, especially in business, science and technology, and petroleum science. Government and business leaders are trying to move nationals into positions that are now held by trained personnel from outside the UAE.

The UAE has a number of universities, including the Higher Colleges of Technology, the Petroleum Institute in Abu Dhabi, and the University of Sharjah. In addition, American University has branches in Dubai and Sharjah, and the British University is located in Dubai.

PROMOTING NEW ROLES FOR WOMEN

One of the leading figures in promoting new roles for women has been Sheikha Fatima bint Mubarak, the widow of Shayk Zayid, the ruler of Abu Dhabi and the architect of the UAE federation in 1971. Her Highness has long believed that education is the key for allowing women to become important contributors to the new nation. In 1975 she started the Abu Dhabi Women's Society and became its first chairperson.

The Society encourages women to be "the builders of the future at the side of their male partner." Women who remain in the home, raising the children, should see themselves as being just as important as women who have business or professional careers.

Early in 2006 Her Highness Sheikha Fatima traveled to Cairo, Egypt, to establish an award designed to encourage all Arab women, not only the women of the Emirates. The award, The Sheikha Fatima Bint Mubarak Award for the Outstanding Arab Woman, is awarded through the Arab Woman's Organization. Each year the award presentation will coincide with Arab Women's Day, on February 1. The purpose of the award is to give public recognition to the unique contributions of women.

RELIGION

FIVE TIMES A DAY THE STREETS of cities in the United Arab Emirates echo with a familiar chant—the Muslim call to worship. The call is given from a tower, or minaret, by a muezzin, located near one of the many mosques (Muslim places of worship). On hearing the muezzin's call, the faithful enter a mosque, take off their shoes, and kneel, facing the holy city of Mecca. Out in the desert, far from any minaret or mosque, a Bedu herder will still pause five times a day to express his faith by removing a small prayer rug from his pack and kneeling on it in the sand.

Ninety-six percent of the citizens of the UAE are Muslim, with 85 percent following the Sunni branch of Islam, and most of the rest adhering to

Opposite: **Jumeirah Mosque is one of the most noted and photographed landmarks in Dubai.**

Below: **An Emirati boy studies verses from the Koran.**

the Shia branch. Although no official figures are available, UN observers estimate that about 55 percent of the expatriate population is Muslim, 25 percent is Hindu, 10 percent is Christian, and 5 percent is Buddhist. Another 5 percent belong to smaller religions, mostly from India, such as Parsiism, Bahaism, and Sikhism.

While conditions differ from one emirate to another, visitors say that the UAE offers more religious freedom than other Gulf states, including Saudi Arabia and Qatar. There are several Christian churches and schools, primarily in Dubai and Abu Dhabi.

ISLAM

The forces that unite the people of the UAE are their Arab culture, including loyalty to family and tribe, and their Muslim religion. The religion of Islam emerged through a series of revelations experienced by the Prophet Muhammad between A.D. 610 and his death in 632. It is a monotheistic religion (belief in one God) and Allah is similar to the God of the Bible or the Torah.

The word Islam means "submission" to the will of Allah. This submission involves all aspects of life. It includes rules for a person's daily conduct and social relationships. These rules for living emerge from the holy book of Islam, the Koran (or, Qu'ran) which contains the word of Allah as revealed to the Prophet Muhammad.

Islam has some beliefs that are similar to Judaism and Christianity, including the acceptance of Old Testament prophets, such as Abraham and Moses. Jesus is also thought of as a prophet, but Muhammad is the last prophet and the one to whom Allah revealed his complete message.

Many Muslims use the "thread test" to distinguish daylight and dark. In the evening, when a black thread is no longer visible, it is night. And at dawn, when a white thread becomes visible, daylight has officially arrived.

Goats from Pakistan are loaded off to be sold in an animal market for the Eid al-Adna festival sacrifice in Sharjah.

Muslims throughout the world are united by their adherence to the Five Articles of Islamic Faith and the practice of the Five Pillars of Islam. The Five Articles of Faith include belief in one God, angels, the revealed books, the prophets, and the Day of Judgment.

The Five Pillars of Islam are public acts of faith, and practicing them is a way of making Muslims known to one another. This creates a feeling of unity among the faithful. The public acts of faith include reciting the profession of faith; answering the five daily calls to collective public prayer; paying the *zakat*, or purification tax to aid the poor; fasting during the daylight hours during the holy month of Ramadan; and making the pilgrimage (or hajj) to Mecca at least once in a person's lifetime, unless prevented by health or finances.

RAMADAN

The month of Ramadan is the most solemn period in the Islamic year, the time during which Muhammad received the words found in the Koran. Ramadan is the ninth month of the Muslim calendar, which means that the exact period of thirty days differs by a few days each year.

During Ramadan Muslims show their obedience to the will of Allah by observing a strict fast during daylight hours. Part of the day is spent in prayer, sometimes in a mosque, sometimes with family. At night Muslims break the fast, usually with family members. The meal can extend far into the night and is interspersed with prayer.

ISLAM IN TODAY'S UAE

Following the discovery of oil and the formation of the federation, the influx of foreigners made the UAE a much larger society, and a multicultural one. Fortunately, the many centuries of exposure to foreigners and ideas has made Emirati tolerant of differences.

Muslim men break their fast together outside a mosque during the month of Ramadan.

One way this tolerance has been displayed is in the willingness to change laws to meet the needs of a pluralistic population. For hundreds of years the emirates had relied on Islamic law in judging both civil and criminal matters. Over the past thirty years new laws have been formulated to deal with civil and commercial practices that do not rely on the more rigid rules and punishments laid down by Islamic law, which is also known as Sharia law. These changes were confirmed by a major decision of the Federal Supreme Court, which ruled that punishments prescribed by Sharia courts could no longer be applied to non-Muslims. This paved the way for non-Muslims to be dealt with under the new civil and criminal codes.

Muslims pray during the month of Ramadan inside a mosque in Dubai.

CHRISTIANITY

The tolerance of Arab nationals extends to other religions. Hindu temples, Christian churches, and other places of worship are respected, with the understanding that no attempt will be made by adherents of these religions to convert others. There are several Christian churches in Abu Dhabi, and Dubai has two large churches: St. Mary's, which is Roman Catholic, and the interdenominational Holy Trinity Church.

The Christian churches follow the same practices as churches in Europe and North America. Some holidays, such as Easter, are based on the lunar calendar, so they fall on different dates every year. Other special days follow the Gregorian calendar, including Christmas (December 25) and New Year's Day (January 1).

HINDUISM

About 25 percent of the UAE's population, including people from parts of India, Pakistan, Sri Lanka, and other South Asian countries, follows Hinduism. There are many different Hindu sects; all are built around a series of texts, written in Sanskrit, in particular the *Bhagavad Gita* ("Song of the Lord"). Central to all the Hindu sects is the belief in an eternal force lying within all beings—an all-embracing reality called Brahma.

The final goal of worship is said to be a coming together of the individual self and the eternal. Related to this concept is the idea of the passing of an individual soul from one life form to another,

also known as reincarnation. A related principle is karma, whereby one's actions bring either good or bad results, either in this life or in a reincarnation. The endless cycle of rebirth keeps the soul trapped until the individual breaks the cycle through one of several paths, such as intense devotion to God or ritual observance.

Followers of Hindu sects usually build small shrines in their homes in addition to a village or community temple. The worshipper, or *puja*, basically treats God as an honored guest who is invited to look with kindness upon the ritual, which consists of carrying an image around the temple, as well as various other actions. Gifts consisting of fruit, flowers, and perfumes are offered in most sects. The purpose of the rites is for individual worshippers to identify with the divine presence.

Christians light candles after Christmas Mass in Dubai.

LANGUAGE

SINCE ONLY ABOUT 20 PERCENT of the people living in the UAE are nationals, the form of Arabic they use, known as Gulf Arabic, is not universally known throughout the emirates. Arabic is the official language, however, and most people pick up enough of the language from signs, the media, and daily business to get by. In addition, many Arabs from other countries in the Middle East live in the emirates, although many have some difficulty with the Gulf Arabic dialect.

English is the second most common language, especially in the three major cities. Another 10 percent of the population speaks Hindi, the major language of India. Persian, the language of Iran, and Urdu, a language from India and Pakistan, are also common.

Opposite: **An Emrati woman reading in the library of the Women's College.**

Below: **Emirati men reading newspapers and chatting in the street.**

Buying snacks in the noisy souk often requires one to gesture in order to get the right thing.

LANGUAGE WITHOUT WORDS

Communication does not always involve words, of course. Various forms of nonverbal communication, such as actions, gestures, or facial expressions, can be remarkably effective in conveying meaning. And gestures or other nonverbal messages that are acceptable in one culture might be read as an insult in another. Most people in the UAE, because of their long exposure to other peoples and cultures, are relaxed about mistakes in nonverbal communication, accepting the gaffs with good humor. In spite of this friendly attitude, there are a few forms of this silent language to be aware of. For example, allowing a host to see the bottom of your feet is considered rude. A similar example of poor form is crossing one leg over the other. Pointing with one's feet, for example when selecting an item to buy, is also a sign of rudeness.

People take off their shoes when entering a mosque and also when entering someone's home. Even if the host says that it is not necessary to remove shoes, the gesture will be appreciated.

Visitors should always accept coffee, tea, or other light refreshments when offered. This is a traditional sign of hospitality or friendship in Bedouin culture, and rejecting the offer could be considered an insult. Even taking one or two sips would probably be satisfactory.

Travel consultants also suggest that visitors to the UAE avoid heaping praise on some ornament or personal possession. According to the Arab saying *baiti baitak*—"My house is your house"—the host is likely to feel obligated to give the item as a gift. This can also place an obligation on the guest to give a gift of comparable value at some future time.

Visitors are also advised to be respectful of Muslim customs. During the holy month of Ramadan, for example, Muslims must refrain from eating or drinking during daylight hours. Out of respect for this practice, visitors should avoid dining in public during the same time.

WRITTEN ARABIC

Arabic is a fascinating language that seems particularly difficult for Westerners to master. The written language is unusual in several ways. One feature that is different from written languages in Europe, the Americas, Africa, and parts of Asia is that it is written across the page from right to left.

Another interesting feature of written Arabic is that the consonants are written on the line, while vowels are added as marks written above or below the line. The alphabet consists of 29 letters. All the letters are consonants except for *a*, *w* (used for a *w* or *u* sound), and *y* (used for *y* or *i* sounds). The short vowels are added by marks above or below the consonants.

In printed Arabic, such as in a newspaper, the short vowels are usually left out, except in important documents, including the Koran. The name Muhammad would therefore appear in print as m-h-m-d. You would need to know the vowels that were not written in order to figure out the pronunciation.

These features make it difficult to create rules for transliterating Arabic—that is, writing its words in our romanized alphabet, and creating a pronunciation guide. The samples used in this book are common to current travel guides.

THE THREE MOST COMMON PHRASES

Visitors to the emirates are struck by how often they hear or themselves repeat the standard greeting:

> *As-salám alaykum*/Peace be with you
> *Waláykum as-salám*/And to you peace (reply)

ARABIC PRONUNCIATION

Different travel and language guides offer various guides for pronouncing letters. The following samples are found in several guides.

Pronounce:

a as in *look*	*kh* as in *loch* (Scottish)
ai as in *eye*	*gh* as in a rolling *r*
ay as in *may*	*dh* as in *the*
i as in *see*	

Double consonants are pronounced twice as long.

The third common expression is *Insh'Allah*, which means "by the will of Allah (or God)." Visiting businesspeople sometimes find this irritating, because they think it sounds evasive. If you were planning a meeting or conference, for example, and your Arab contacts frequently responded to a suggestion by saying *Insh'Allah*, you might wonder if they were trying to put you off. The frequent use of the term reflects Muslim traditions, as do many aspects of the Arabic language. Not saying the phrase might suggest that the person feels he or she has control over the future when, in fact, it actually will be whatever God decides.

SAMPLE WORDS AND PHRASES

Hello or Welcome	*Márhaba* or *ahlan*
[Reply]	*áhlayn*
Good morning	*Sabáh al-kháyr*
[Reply]	*Sabáh an-núr*
	(may you have a morning of light)
How are you?	*Kâyf hálak?* (to a man)
	Kâyf hálik? (to a woman)
Fine, thank you.	*Zayn, al-hámdu, lillah*
Please	*min fádlak* (to a man)
	min fádlik (to a woman)
Yes	*Náam* or *áiwa*
No	*La*
Excuse me	*Samáhli*
My name is . . .	*Esmi*
What is your name?	*Shú ismak* (to a man)
	ismik (woman)
I am from the United States.	*Ána min Amerika*

ARTS

THROUGHOUT THE LONG HISTORY OF the United Arab Emirates, life was so hard that crafts and most arts were engaged in primarily for practical purposes. A dhow might have elaborate carving, but it was first and foremost an item for transportation. Similarly, weapons, tools, pottery, wind towers, and other crafted items often displayed the skill and artistry of the craftworker, but the primary concern was their function.

Even with the emphasis on practicality, however, there has always been a strong impulse to create something beautiful for its own sake. This creative drive is clearly displayed in activities such as making jewelry and in henna painting to enhance personal beauty. This is also shown in the art used to decorate the Koran.

Since the formation of the federation in 1971, there has been growing interest in restoring and preserving the country's artistic heritage. Abu Dhabi

Left: **Visitors look at art work displayed at a modern and contemporary art sale in Dubai.**

Opposite: **An elderly man plays the drums for a dance performance.**

Men also use henna, following the statement in the Hadith that men should use only henna to dye their hair and beards.

has taken the lead in this effort by opening galleries, sponsoring exhibits, and creating the Heritage Village outside al-'Ayn. Sharjah has also become involved with efforts such as the start of a heritage museum at al-Arsah souk. Dubai has helped private groups, such as the Dubai Art Society, by offering courses in painting, ceramics, photography, and other fields.

HENNA SKIN-DYEING

One of the skills used merely for the creation of beauty is dyeing hands—and often feet, ankles, and wrists—with the natural dye henna. This has been a favorite beautification technique among women of the emirates for centuries. Beauty clinics today in Ra's al-Khaymah and in Dubai City offer henna-dyeing services, which have become popular with tourists.

An Emirati woman applying henna skin-dye to a customer.

The artistry is in the creation of beautifully intricate designs. Floral patterns are common, and so are abstract designs. These are usually applied to the hands as a beauty treatment. Henna dyeing is also associated with weddings. During the bride-to-be's prenuptial pampering, the patterns are applied to her wrists, ankles, and feet.

HENNA HAND-PAINTING

The red dye called henna is used in the traditional craft of hand-painting. Hand-painting is done on any special occasion, especially marriage. It is increasingly popular with tourists.

The leaves of the henna shrub are ground into a fine powder using a mortar and pestle. This is then strained through a muslin cloth. The smooth powder is mixed with eucalyptus oil and lemon juice to make a paste.

The henna paste is applied to the hands or feet in intricate designs, usually floral. Brides-to-be often have their hands, feet, wrists, and ankles decorated several days before the wedding ceremony.

Beauty clinics will do hand-painting for clients. The henna decorations can soften the skin and cool it against the harsh sunlight. The rich pigment can last on the skin for several weeks.

Traditional weaving is done using a very simple loom.

WEAVING

Even in the harsh desert environment, Bedu women display remarkable skill and artistry in weaving. They weave on very simple looms, with the wool spooled around a wooden shuttle, which is then passed between the warp threads stretched between two wooden sticks. Traditionally, the women used only natural dyes, such as sulfur, shells, and plants, including henna. In the past fifty years artificial dyes have become common and produce brighter colors.

With few animals, nomadic women use their resources carefully. Sheep's wool is generally used for furnishings and small rugs, while goat's wool is used mostly for tent cloth.

The patterns created are often strikingly beautiful, with geometric designs or stylized shapes of familiar objects. Patterns are extended to the edge of the fabric rather than to a border. This is said to symbolize the endless horizon of the desert. The largest woven piece is the tent curtain. This is usually black and white, with the white being cotton purchased through trade. The curtain is narrow and runs from the back wall to the front, making a divider that provides privacy for the women.

In an effort to preserve traditional crafts, both government and private agencies have established cultural centers, where crafts such as weaving are demonstrated, and lessons are offered.

CULTURAL HERITAGE CENTERS

The Dubai International Arts Center in Jumeirah is one of the oldest private groups devoted to promoting traditional arts and crafts. Started in 1976, the center offers regular courses and demonstrations in both traditional and nontraditional forms, such as interior decorating, photography, and painting. There is also a course in Gulf Arabic. The city of Dubai has provided two beach villas to the center, allowing it to expand its operations.

In spite of the increasing interest, many of the craft items available for purchase are not indigenous but rather imported from other countries. The Emirati have been importing craft items since the earliest days of maritime trade, and this trade continues in the present. Tourists shopping in the souks bargain for such things as carpets from Iran, metalware from India, and jewelry from Oman. Many of the items are antiques.

Examples of older items made in the UAE are found primarily in museums. Emirate governments have established a number of heritage centers that, like the Dubai International Arts Center, provide courses and demonstrations. These centers are said to be the best sites for purchasing and learning about contemporary arts and crafts.

An Emirati craftsman makes traditional daggers at a hunting show in Abu Dhabi.

ARTISTRY IN WEAPONS

Weapons were very important to Bedu men, not only as tools for fighting but as symbols of their family, clan, and tribe. They took great care of their weapons, using wet sand to keep them clean and free of rust, and even bestowing their favorites with pet names.

Swords and daggers were two of the most popular weapons to decorate elaborately. The short, curved dagger called a *khanjar* had intricate decorations and was carried in a silver scabbard. These are still worn by some men for special occasions. There are also several different sizes and shapes of daggers with handles made of ivory or horn, with decorations made of gold or silver.

By the 19th century rifles and revolvers were important weapons. Revolver handles and rifle butts were elaborately carved or had stone inlays. Bows and arrows, including crossbows, were often decorated with seashell inlays.

JEWELRY: BETTER THAN A BANK

Most of the jewelry worn by Emirati women or sold in the souks, is made in Oman and other countries. An exception is the practice among Bedu women of creating their own pieces out of coins, chains, beads, and other items purchased from village jewelers or from traveling merchants, including hajj pilgrims. Nearly all this jewelry is worn by women and children.

In the past silver was the most highly valued form of jewelry, because it had the greatest value. Women wore chains containing coins with a high silver content. Since the late 19th century gold has become the favored metal, and it is also a major medium of international exchange. In Dubai and Abu Dhabi, entire souks are filled with shops dealing in gold jewelry.

Traditionally, women own the jewelry they wear, but they can also act as the family's bank, because many nomadic families prefer to convert any money they have into jewelry rather than putting it in a bank.

DHOW BUILDING

The ancient craft of dhow-building has gone through several changes. Dhows were used for fishing, trade, and pearling for hundreds of years, each boat carefully made by hand. Some craftworkers on Dubai Creek and the outskirts of 'Ajman continue to build them the traditional way. They work with wood and use the simplest hand tools, such as planes, adzes, and chisels. Without using blueprints, the builders hand saw the main ribs out of single pieces of wood.

In the early years of the oil boom it seemed likely that dhows would become obsolete, replaced by more modern vessels. However, the ruling family of Dubai launched a revival of dhow-racing, and that triggered a new interest in the boats.

Changes in technology have also kept the craft alive. Fiberglass has become popular, replacing the wooden hulls, because it is lighter and more durable. Many modern dhows are also equipped with diesel engines as well as navigation aids such as radios and radar.

A NAME FOR EVERYTHING

The Gulf Arabs' fondness for practicality is displayed in their practice of giving a name to every handcrafted item that describes its precise function. In pottery, for example, pots called *al-khers* are for storing food, *al-jarrah* are for carrying water from a well, *al-borma* are for cooking, *al-masaab* are for holding coffee, and *al-razem* are for holding or carrying coffee cups. There is also a special name—*al-haalool*—for vessels for giving water to wildlife.

The same precision is applied to items made from date palm leaves. *Al-makhrafah*, for instance, is a container in which dates are collected, while *al-mezmah* is used to carry dates home, and *al-jefeer* are containers used to carry dates to market.

Dhows have been made in all sizes. The largest design, called a boom, had several large sails and was used for ocean trade to India and beyond. Some ancient booms have been converted into colorful, two-story restaurants. Smaller dhows, used in coastal trade, usually had a single, large, billowing sail, and a smaller one. Some had a raised deck, under which was a small cabin for the captain and crew. Others were completely open, with a canopy stretched the length of the deck to protect the cargo, and sometimes the crew, from sun or rain.

A dhow being built using traditional methods.

POTTERY

The people of what is now the UAE have been making pottery for more than 4,000 years. Vessels made out of the local red clay have traditionally been fired in a stone kiln lined with mud. Most of the pottery is made in Ra's al-Khaymah; some have also been imported from Oman and Iran.

Most of the pottery is quite plain and utilitarian, so it has not been a great attraction to tourists. Government efforts to revive the craft and create public exhibits have had modest success.

Opposite: **Emirati musicians celebrate an event with traditional musical instruments.**

Below: **A potter demonstrates his skill at an UAE heritage village.**

MUSIC

In the hard life of the desert people, song and dance provided welcome relief from hardship and monotony. Some of the music expresses strong emotions, while other songs are made up of complex religious chants. Traditional music can still be heard on special occasions, such as at weddings or celebrations of National Day (December 2).

A wide variety of musical instruments were made from materials found in the desert or along the coast. Percussion instruments included the *jaser*, a drum made of goat skin on a wooden frame, which was hung around the neck. The *nisk* was made of coastal materials—a coconut sound box decorated with shells. The *sheklelah* was a tambourinelike

A number of UAE singers have become popular throughout the Persian Gulf. Ahlam is considered the first Arab female pop star. Other popular singers are Samar, Reem, and Abdallah Belkhair.

The UAE does not yet have a strong literary tradition, in large because there was not a literate audience until the past two or three decades. That is beginning to change, and a number of writers have become the pioneers of a new literary age. Mohammed al-Murr, for example, has emerged as one of the UAE's leading fiction writers. His book, *The Wink of the Mona Lisa*, is a collection of twenty-four short stories. In addition, a number of leading figures have written about the country's economic miracle, including Mohammed al-Fahim's *From Rags to Riches, A Story of Abu Dhabi*.

Poetry is part of the emirates' long oral tradition dating back more than a thousand years. Verses were recited in a singsong voice or sung, often accompanied by musical instruments. As with music and dance, poetry is often centred around religion.

instrument made of cloth and goat hooves and tied around the waist so that it clattered as the wearer moved. There were also wind instruments: one was a metal pipe wrapped with bands of copper, another was a bamboo pipe with two rows of holes. There was also a rosewood pipe wrapped with silver thread. Perhaps the most unusual instrument was a bagpipe made of goat skin, with a bamboo mouthpiece and goat hair tassels on the pipe. String instruments included a harplike instrument, made of wood and animal skin, and a simple wood violin.

Except for use on special occasions, these instruments have been replaced by electronic guitars and synthesizers. Night clubs and hotels organize special evenings of Arabic music. These events, which often run all night, also include more modern Middle Eastern songs. Usually, the audience becomes involved, dancing with their hands in the air. Belly dancing, which originated in Egypt, is also popular.

DANCE

Both music and dance strengthen the sense of belonging to a family, a clan, and a tribe. Some dances were used on the eve of war, even though warfare was usually in the form of a raid, rather than large battles.

Because of the region's long history of maritime trade, dances have been introduced from other parts of the world. For example, a dance called the *lewa* originated in Africa. It uses large drums and has a very fast tempo.

A variety of folk dances were performed on special occasions, including weddings, and traditionally on the return of the pearl divers. Some dances are related to Islam, including adaptations of narratives about the life of Muhammad.

A folklore troop performs a traditional dance in Dubai.

105

LEISURE

THE PEOPLE OF THE UNITED Arab Emirates are well aware of how the country's oil wealth has transformed their way of life, and they are deeply grateful. This is the first generation to have leisure time and enough money to enjoy it. They are joined in these cheerful pursuits by thousands of visitors. Some foreigners come to combine business with pleasure; others come for family vacations, and a growing number are purchasing vacation homes in the UAE, especially on the new palm-shaped islands.

This small country has a great climate for leisure pursuits. The only drawback to the sun-filled climate is that the summer heat is so oppressive that people tend to avoid it as much as possible. The oil wealth has provided many alternatives, including air-conditioned malls, theaters, and restaurants, as well as shaded parks, fountains, and pools.

FAMILY LEISURE

A good deal of people's leisure time involves traditional activities mixed with the new and modern. Social visits remain a favorite pastime, for example, almost always involving coffee or tea and often light refreshments. While these visits usually take place in someone's home, the availability of air-conditioned cafés and coffee shops offers an inviting new way to get together.

Families also take advantage of the variety of parks, green spaces, and pools scattered throughout the cities. Many parks have family-oriented features, such as barbecue pits, play areas for children, and

Above: **An Emirati father and son playing on Jumeirah Beach.**

Opposite: **A group of Emrati men enjoying a game of beach volleyball on Jumeira Beach.**

107

Shoppers in the Mall of Emiratis in Dubai.

swimming pools with lifeguards. Beaches are also a favorite gathering place for families. The beautiful sand beaches extend for miles, and many are equipped with beach umbrellas or palm trees for shade. Jumeirah Beach is reserved for women and children on certain days, and Al-Dana Beach is solely for women and children.

SHOPPING

The three major cities are rapidly making the UAE one of the world's greatest shopping centers. Dubai even has an annual shopping festival.

An almost endless array of goods is available, from the latest electronic marvels to antique copperware and Oriental rugs. While locally made crafts are hard to find, there is an abundance from throughout Southern Asia. There are also designer shops, featuring labels from Paris, London, and New York. The malls and shops are open early and close late. Most close for three hours during the hottest part of the day.

A more traditional kind of shopping takes place in the souks, where narrow alleys lead to merchant shops and stalls. Many people prefer shopping in the souks, partly because they are reminders of a proud history, and some like the fun of haggling over prices. In addition, shoppers may chance upon unique items, and there are tailor shops that can re-create any article of expensive designer clothing at a fraction of the cost.

AMUSEMENT PARKS

In their bid to bring tourist dollars to the UAE while also providing fun for nationals, the emirates have created several colossal amusement parks. Dubai has led the way with the Wonder Land Theme and Water Park, featuring water slides and a number of large rides with varying levels of thrill. Dubai claims it to be the largest amusement park in the world.

Not to be outdone, Umm al-Qaywayan has built Dreamland Aqua Park. It has twenty water slides and an enormous children's pool.

Spectators attend Dubai Desert Classic at Emirates Golf Club.

A NEW AGE IN SPORTS

In February 2006 hundreds of spectators lined the course as golf great Tiger Woods stormed from behind to tie for the lead and then win the tournament in a one-hole playoff. The tournament was the Dubai Desert Classic, which now draws some of the worlds' best golfers.

Golf is just one of many sports that is rapidly gaining popularity. The people of the emirates, as well as foreign visitors, are taking advantage of the wide array of sports facilities becoming available. Some of the

AN AMAZING GOLF PROJECT

In November 2005 land was auctioned to private homeowners to launch a remarkable new golf project a few miles outside Dubai City. The project, called Jumeirah Golf Estates (JGE), will have 946 homeowners in Phase A, and about the same in Phase B.

Dinah Al Jaflah, general manager of JGE, said that the project will include four golf courses, built around the themes of Fire, Earth, Wind, and Water. These environmentally friendly courses will contain native plants. There will also be community centers, tennis clubs, swimming pools, commercial and retail outlets, schools, and a medical center. Families from the UAE, Europe, and the United States have quickly bought up the home lots on this upscale sports facility.

sports are traditional. Others, such as golf, are new to the UAE, and are inviting to spectators as well as participants.

HORSE RACING

Sheikh Mohammed, the president of Dubai, is typical of the new generation of sports enthusiasts, loving both the traditional and the new. A man of many talents, he has the reputation of being a good ruler with ambitious plans for his emirate. He has written poetry; and gained an international reputation in the sport of endurance racing, taking part in 70-mile (112-km) horse-racing marathons across the desert. The entire al-Maktoum family, rulers of Dubai, has taken a leading role in promoting horse racing. The family members want the UAE to be a center for Thoroughbred training and racing. They point out that every Thoroughbred horse racing today can trace its lineage to Arabian stallions, which were exported to Britain three centuries ago.

Today, the $4 million Dubai World Cup is the richest horse race in the world. The family has spent more than $2 billion in establishing the Al Quoz Stables and in improving training facilities. They have built a great racing complex with a stadium, a grass track and a sand track, and a golf course in the enormous infield. The al-Maktoums have some 1,500 thoroughbreds training in Europe and North America, as well as in Dubai.

Most golf courses in desert regions offer only patches of grass. The rest of it is sand. At many desert courses golfers place a small green mat on the sand, place their ball on it, and swing. At most UAE courses, however, desalinated water and electronically controlled sprinklers create luxurious green fairways.

The Dubai World Cup is the world's richest horse race with a first prize of $6 million.

The UAE's interest in horseback riding is not limited to the high-profile races. There are several smaller racetracks scattered throughout the country. In addition, there are many facilities for horseback riding, including places offering lessons for beginners.

CAMEL RACING

Camel racing is another sport with a long history that has experienced a new flurry of interest in the UAE. The sport is popular throughout the country, with races run on both circular and straight tracks. The races, held on Fridays and public holidays, are noisy affairs because supporters drive behind the camels in four-wheel-drive vehicles to urge them on.

Training is often put in the hands of Bedu, who specialize in breeding and training racing camels. They prepare the camels for the racing season, which runs from September to late April, and each trainer feeds his animals a special concoction, usually including alfalfa, barley, ghee (clarified butter), honey, and dates.

The jockeys are usually children, because of their light weight. Children as young as six or seven are riders, even though the camels reach speeds of 37 miles per hour (60 kph). The lure of winning prize money draws many children to try out as jockeys.

Young camel jockeys take part in a camel race in Dubai.

FALCONRY

Falconry has been a favorite sport of desert sheikhs for many centuries. Falcons have been trained to hunt doves, sandgrouse, and the houbara bustard. The sport is even more popular today among the wealthy. Falcon clubs for exercising and training the handsome, intelligent birds are found on the outskirts of every city and town.

The hunting season lasts from October to January, which is also the time of autumn bird migrations. Falcons are purchased from Iran, Pakistan, and other countries at prices that range from $320 to $30,000; the price depends on several factors, including the length of the tail

feathers, an indicator of flying ability. Females, being one-third larger than males, are generally preferred.

The standard equipment for falconry includes the leather glove, or *mangalah*, worn by the falconer for protection against the bird's sharp talons. When resting, the falcon perches on a *wakir*, a highly decorated pole, and the head is covered with a leather hood called a burka.

Hunting expeditions have always been elaborate affairs organized by sheikhs and consist of 20 or more people. Most trips are now made in four-wheel-drive vehicles. Once bird tracks are identified, a camp is set up, and the hunters go to work. The falcons are incredibly swift, and the largest species, the saker, uses its keen intelligence to predict the movements of its prey and uses the landscape to disguise its own movements.

OTHER SPECTATOR SPORTS

Several other sports are geared toward spectators as well as participants. Some sports have been promoted in Dubai to draw sports enthusiasts from around the world. In addition to the golf tournament, the emirate hosts the Dubai Tennis Championships and the Dubai World Cup in golf, bringing the world's top tennis players and professional golfers to the UAE. For participants, tennis courts and golf courses are available throughout the emirates.

The Dubai Open attracts top players to the emirates to pit their skills against one another.

BULLFIGHTING

Because the terrain of al-Fujayrah, the easternmost emirate, is not conducive for camel racing, bullfighting has long been a popular substitute as a spectator sport. This is not bullfighting in the style of Spain or Mexico, in which a lone matador confronts a bull. Instead, this is a contest of one 2,000-pound Brahma bull fighting another.

The bulls, long used for work in the emirate's palm groves, are bred for strength and raised on a diet of grain, honey, and milk. The goal of the fight is for one bull to force the other to the ground. A bull can also win by forcing its opponent to flee.

The age of the sport is unknown. The bulls may have been introduced by the Portuguese in the 16th century, but the sport itself may date back to before A.D. 1000 in Persia.

A number of smaller events are useful for introducing the people of Dubai to new sports. Car races, bowling championships, football (called soccer in the United States), and rugby are all available. Some sporting developments are unusual. Sharjah, for example, has been host to the World Masters cricket tournament. Ice-skating rinks are becoming increasingly popular, and ice hockey is emerging as a new spectator sport.

WATER SPORTS

The clear waters of the Gulf and its eternal sunshine invite an amazing variety of water sports. Other water sports include sailing, surfing and windsurfing, snorkeling, and water-skiing. There has also been a revival of dhow racing. The rulers of the UAE organize several races, including the annual President's Cup Regatta, which is also known as the Dubai-Muscat Offshore Sailing Race. There are also a variety of dhow excursions for fishing, scuba diving, or dolphin watches.

Sailing at Jumeirah Beach, Dubai.

FESTIVALS

EMIRATI CELEBRATE A VARIETY OF holidays, both secular and religious. The influx of people from other parts of the world, who now account for about 80 percent of the population, have brought along a number of immigrants with their own special observances.

Because of the country's brief history as a nation, there are few secular holidays commemorating historical events. One exception is National Day, celebrated on December 2, as the day the constitution was approved to create the federation of the seven emirates. The day is marked with fireworks, fairs, and sporting events, such as horse races.

In addition, several of the emirates have special days to honor their ruling sheikh. For many years, for example, Abu Dhabi marked August 6 as a holiday, celebrating the accession of Shayk Zayid. New Year's Day—January 1—is also a secular holiday. The Islamic New Year follows the lunar calendar, so it falls a few days earlier each year.

Above: **A group of entertainers at the opening of the Dubai Summer Surprises Festival.**

Opposite: **Emrati men playing drums during a celebration in Dubai.**

FAMILY CELEBRATIONS

As in other cultures, family festivals follow major events in the life cycle—birthdays, marriage, the birth of children, and death. There are numerous traditions associated with these events, many of them stemming from Bedu desert life, others from Islamic practices.

Marriage announcements are issued verbally by women, while men announce the event in the mosque. The Bedu tradition of hospitality is highlighted in the wedding feast. Separate dining tents are established for

A family in Abu Dhabi. Better medical facilities now have seen a significant decrease in infant mortality rates.

men and women, and a special kitchen is set up to prepare mountains of food. Guests are encouraged to take away food parcels to give to any friends or relatives who could not attend.

The birth of a child is also an occasion for great celebration. Births take place in the modern, well-equipped hospitals located throughout the UAE. The hospital births have greatly reduced the previously high infant mortality rate, and families have adjusted their celebrations to fit the new hospital environment. Visitors now bring their presents and special foods to the hospital, and the halls are filled with colorful bouquets. All the new mothers and families on the same ward congratulate each other, even though they have probably never met before.

For Muslims death is usually not an occasion for extended mourning. If possible, the deceased is buried on the day of death, with the body placed on its side, facing Mecca. Forty days after death close family members hold a feast to celebrate the deceased's ascent into heaven.

ISLAMIC FESTIVALS

Islam has a number of holidays throughout the year. These generally follow the Islamic calendar, which is based on the phases of the moon, so their dates change by a few days each year.

The most important period in Islam is the month of Ramadan, the ninth month in the lunar calendar. Faithful Muslims observe a strict fast every day of the month during daylight hours. After sunset there are dinners, prayers, and business meetings that can extend far into the night. These evenings are also important times for majlis, when citizens can express their views to their ruler or petition him for some special act or favor.

Fridays are the days of rest in Islam, much as Sundays are in Christianity and Saturdays are in Judaism. Muslims attend services in their mosques, and most businesses are closed.

Muslims at a mosque in Dubai praying during the holy month of Ramadan.

Dates are considered a favorable food to end the day of fasting at sunset during Ramadan.

The month of Ramadan is followed by a great festival called 'Id al-Fitr, the Feast of the Fast Breaking, held during the first four days of the month of Shawwal. People enjoy festive meals, exchange gifts, take part in family or community prayers, and hold important business meetings. This is another time for majlis, when tribal leaders and business executives visit the people who depend on them to resolve any problems.

Other Islamic holidays include the ascension of the Prophet, the Prophet's birthday, and the Islamic New Year. Another festival, 'Id al-Adha, takes place during the month of the hajj—the pilgrimage to Mecca.

FESTIVE MEALS

Great feasts are part of most festivals in the UAE. Frequently, the meals center around what is called *ouzi*, meaning "live cooking." This usually consists of fresh lamb, cooked outdoors on a spit or in an oven until the meat is very tender. The lamb can be stuffed with a mixture of rice, spices, raisins, and nuts.

A tradition for any special occasion is the *fou-alla*, consisting of a platter of delicate sweets, served with coffee or tea. The meal ends with women burning a variety of incense.

HINDU FESTIVALS

The large Hindu population, made up of immigrants from India, celebrates a variety of occasions. These vary according to what part of India the people came from. Many of the festivals include religious ceremonies mixed with processions, demonstrations of magic, feasting, and a number of fun-filled activities. During the spring Holi festival, for example, which is designed to revive the powers of nature, participants throw colored powder and water at each other.

In festivals celebrating the New Year, also normally held in spring, objects representing the sickness and "impurities" of the past year are thrown into a bonfire. People also celebrate the coming of the New Year by forgiving debts owed to them, paying their own debts, and trying to resolve any lingering conflicts or problems. In one variation of New Year celebrations, ceremonial lights honor Laksmi, the goddess of wealth and good fortune. During the days of this October festival fireworks are lit to chase away evil spirits, and people engage in several kinds of gambling, which is designed to bring good luck.

The colorful Holi festival, also known as the festival of colors is enthusiastically celebrated by Hindu believers.

FOOD

THE FOOD OF THE UNITED Arab Emirates has become a remarkable buffet of cuisine from throughout the world. This mixing of foods and recipes emerged partly from the region's long history of international trade. The oil boom brought many immigrants from India, Pakistan, and the Philippines, with each group bringing its own special tastes and traditions. In addition, the emergence of a large tourism industry has added all sorts of Western cuisines, including French, Italian, and fast foods from the United States.

Although it is difficult to identify a distinct UAE cuisine, certain traditions have remained. Many of these traditions emerged from the Bedu lifestyle. The Bedu, for example, ate from a communal plate, using the right hand. This form of communal eating, which is also sanctioned by the teachings of the Prophet, is common throughout the Arab world.

Above: **Basmati rice is known for its fragrance and can be only cultivated in the Indian subcontinent.**

Opposite: **Spices, key ingredients in Middle Eastern cooking, on sale in an old spice souk in Deira, Dubai.**

TRADITIONAL UAE FOOD

Before the changes introduced by the oil boom, Emirati families ate the foods available to them, including several imported items, such as basmati rice from Pakistan. Fish, lamb, goat, and dates were standard. Meat was cooked on a grill or barbecue and seasoned with local spices, including cardamom, cumin, and coriander. Other imported flavorings were chili, ginger, cinnamon, nutmeg, and saffron.

One of the unique flavors of traditional cooking was imparted by dried limes. These imported limes, found in Oman and Asian countries such as Thailand, are dried on the tree and are still used in many recipes.

The diet of the nomadic Bedu relied heavily on the camel. They drank camel milk hot, cold, or boiled with bread. It could also be cooked with rice. They ate meat occasionally, usually by trading for goat meat. Near the coast they could purchase fresh or dried fish, such as sun-dried sardines.

DAILY MEALS

Oil wealth has made possible the importation of a wide range of fresh fruits and vegetables. The governments of the emirates have also devoted sizable resources to increasing domestic food production, including fruits, eggs, and dairy products.

A typical breakfast, or *fatoor*, is likely to consist of fresh fruit or juice, eggs, pita (unleavened Arabic bread), jam or honey, and coffee or tea. Lunch (*ghu daa*) is the main meal of the day. Fish, chicken, or meat is usually served with rice and fresh herbs, followed by dates and other fruits. Dinner, or *aa sha*, is a lighter meal of pita bread and cheese or meat, eggs or soup, followed by fruit and tea or coffee.

THE COFFEE CEREMONY

The traditional UAE coffee, called *kahwa*, is offered to guests as a symbol of hospitality and is also an important component of midday meals. The traditional method of preparing coffee involves roasting the beans in a frying pan, then grinding them with a mortar and pestle, and boiling them. Today it is quite acceptable to buy coffee that has already been roasted and ground. The boiled coffee is poured over a mixture of cardamom, cloves, and saffron, creating a light, fairly sweet and aromatic coffee.

Coffee is poured from a pot called a *dallah* and is served in tiny cups without handles. After having two or three cups, it is acceptable to refuse another refill, normally by shaking the cup from side to side. Men often share a *shisha*, or hookah pipe afterwards, although the government is discouraging this for health reasons.

Traditional coffee shops seem to be disappearing, replaced by modern European and American coffee houses. A few of the old-style shops are still found in the souks, and the coffee ceremony is still practiced in people's homes.

DINING OUT

Many of the UAE's restaurants, including those in posh hotels, serve buffets for both lunch and dinner. This style is common throughout the Middle East, especially in Lebanese restaurants, which are very popular in the emirates.

Lebanese restaurants usually serve a dazzling array of 25 to 30 small dishes with dips, called meze. These are followed by a main course, but many diners limit themselves to meze.

Several meze dishes are extremely popular. Tabbouleh, for example, is an herb salad made with bulgur wheat, mixed with chopped parsley, onions, tomato, and mint. Hummus is also popular, it is a paste made of mashed chickpeas mixed with tahini (sesame and garlic paste), olive oil,

Tabbouleh is a favorite of Emiratis and staple meze dish.

and lemon juice, sometimes topped with minced lamb. Another delicious dish is *moutabel*, which is made from eggplant.

All of these dips or spreads are eaten with pita bread or a variation called *mafrooda*, an almost-white bread, without a pocket, which is held in the right hand and used as a scoop to pick up the meze. A variety of fresh vegetables is also available for picking up the dips.

The main course usually consists of chicken or lamb kebabs. Many kinds of fish are also cut into chunks and served as kebabs. Prawns and other forms of seafood are also common.

INTERNATIONAL VARIETIES

In the tourist-oriented cities of the UAE, almost every form of international cuisine is available. The four- and five-star hotels offer European and North American foods, including French, Italian, German, Hungarian, and American Creole, as well as Mexican.

Abu Dhabi, Dubai, and Sharjah also have more modestly priced restaurants featuring the cuisines of India, Pakistan, Thailand, and the Philippines. In addition, Arabic restaurants offer such specialties as *shawarma*, chicken, beef, or lamb roasted on a spit, and falafel, patties made of ground chickpeas and served with pita pockets.

FAST FOODS

There are many different fast foods available in the UAE. The Arabic *shawarma* can be topped with yogurt or tahini and served in a pita pocket, to be eaten like a sandwich. Falafel, too, is often sold by street vendors and served in a paper bag.

European and American fast foods are also popular. Hamburgers, pizza, fish and chips, and other foods typical of American restaurant chains are available in the shopping malls of the three major cities. The towns of the smaller emirates, such as Ra's al-Khaymah, Fujayrah, and Umm al-Qaywayan, have not embraced fast foods.

McDonald's and KFC fast food restaurants are common in the developed cities such as Dubai and Abu Dhabi.

GULF COUSCOUS SALAD

There are many variations of this basic couscous salad. It takes less than 30 minutes to make, but it is best when chilled overnight. Serves 4–6.

1½ cups couscous (uncooked)
2 cups water (or combine 1 cup water and 1 cup chicken broth)
½ teaspoon salt
¼ teaspoon black pepper
2 tablespoons lemon juice
3 tablespoons olive oil
2 large tomatoes, chopped
1 medium zucchini, cut in half and thinly sliced
½ cup fresh basil, cut into strips
⅓ cup scallions, sliced
¾ cup feta cheese, crumbled

Place water, salt, and pepper in a medium saucepan and bring just to a boil. Stir in couscous and cover. Remove from heat and let stand for 5 minutes. Fluff couscous lightly with a fork. Spoon the cooked couscous into a large bowl. Lightly stir in lemon juice and olive oil. Add tomatoes, zucchini, basil, and scallions. Chill in refrigerator overnight, or for at least four hours. Before serving, stir in feta cheese. For variety, add 2 tablespoons of tomato juice, 2 teaspoons of fresh dill (or 1 teaspoon dried dill), and ¼ cup of sliced black olives.

ARABIAN DATE BARS

The different ways of preparing dates are almost endless, and these tasty date bars are one of the best. Makes about 3½ dozen.

1 cup sugar
3 eggs
⅞ cups of flour
1 teaspoon baking powder
⅛ teaspoon salt
1 teaspoon vanilla
2 cups dates, chopped
1 cup walnuts or pecans, chopped
1 cup confectioners' sugar

Preheat the oven to 325°F (163°C). Break the eggs into a mixing bowl. Slowly sift sugar into beaten eggs. Sift flour into a 2-cup measuring cup to measure ⅞ cup. Sift flour again with baking powder and salt. Add sifted ingredients to egg mixture. Add vanilla, and beat until well blended. Stir in dates and nuts. Grease and flour a 9 x 13 inch baking pan. Pour in batter and bake for 25 minutes. Allow date-nut sheet to cool for 20–30 minutes, then cut into bars. Roll the bars in confectioners' sugar and serve. Wrap leftover bars in wax paper.

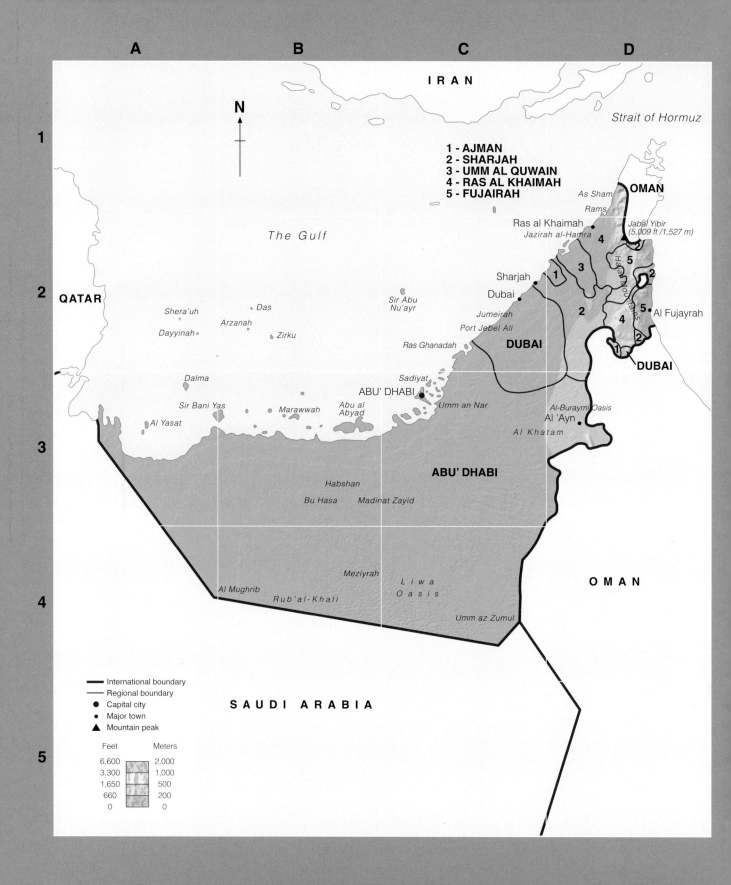

MAP OF UNITED ARAB EMIRATES

Abu al Abyad, B3

Abu Dhabi, A3–A4, B3–B4, C2–C4, D3

Ajman, D2

Al-'Ayn, D3

Al-Buraymi Oasis, D3

Al Fujayrah, D2

Al Khatam, C3, D3

Al Mughrib, B4

Al Yasat, A3

As Sham, D1

Arzanah, B2

Bu Hasa, B3

Dalma, A3

Das, B2

Dayyinah, A2

Dubai, C2–C3, D2, D3

Fujairah, D2

Habsan, B3

Hajar Mountains, D2

Iran, B1, C1, D1

Jabal Yibir, D2

Jazirah al-Hamra, D2

Jumeirah, C2

Liwa Oasis, B4, C4

Madinat Zayid, B3

Marawwah, B3

Meziyrah, B4

Oman, D1–D5, C4

Port Jebel Ali, C2

Qatar, A1, A2

Rams, D1

Ras Al Khaimah, D1-D2

Ras Ghanadah, C2

Rub 'al-Khali, B4

Sadiyat, C3

Saudi Arabia, A3–A5, B4–B5, C4–C5, D4–D5

Sharjah, C2, D2–D3, C3

Shera'uh, A2

Sir Abu Nu'ayr, C2

Sir Bani Yas, A3, B3

Strait of Hormuz, D1

The Gulf, A1–A3, B1–B3, C1–C3, D1–D2

Umm Al Quwain, D2

Umm an Nar, C3

Umm az Zumul, C4

Zirku, B2

ECONOMIC
UNITED ARAB EMIRATES

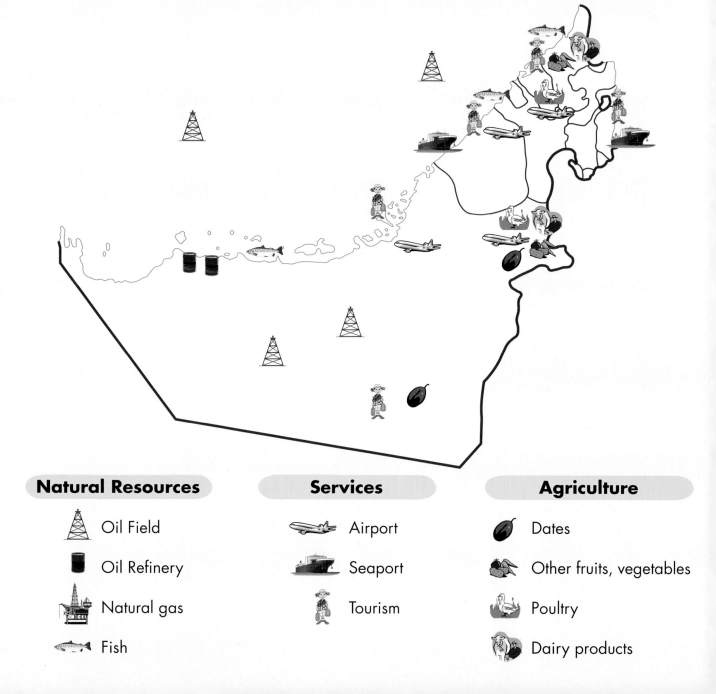

Natural Resources

- Oil Field
- Oil Refinery
- Natural gas
- Fish

Services

- Airport
- Seaport
- Tourism

Agriculture

- Dates
- Other fruits, vegetables
- Poultry
- Dairy products

ABOUT
THE ECONOMY

GROSS DOMESTIC PRODUCT
$63.7 billion (2004 est.)

PER CAPITA GDP
$25,200

GDP GROWTH RATE
5.7 percent

GDP BY SECTOR
Agriculture 4 percent; industry 58.5 percent; services 37.5 percent

AGRICULTURAL PRODUCTS
Dates, other fruits, vegetables, poultry, eggs, dairy products, fish

INDUSTRIAL PRODUCTS
Oil refining, aluminum, textiles, petrochemicals, handicrafts, boats

INFLATION RATE
4.5 percent (2005 estimate)

CURRENCY
Dirham (AED)
USD 1 = 3.67 Dirham

WORKFORCE
2.36 million

WORKFORCE BY SECTOR
Agriculture 7 percent; industry 15 percent; services 78 percent

UNEMPLOYMENT RATE
2.4 percent (2002)

MAIN EXPORTS
Crude oil, natural gas, dates, dried fish

MAIN IMPORTS
Machinery, transportation equipment, chemicals, food

MAIN TRADE PARTNERS
Japan, India, China, Iran, Germany, United Kingdom, United States, South Korea, Iran

CULTURAL
UNITED ARAB EMIRATES

The Ajman Museum
Located in a late 18th century fort and former ruler's palace; includes a reconstructed barasti home.

Dreamland
One of the world's largest aqua parks.

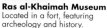

Ras al-Khaimah Museum
Located in a fort, featuring archeology and history.

Sheikh Saeed Al-Maktoum House
A restored ruler's house, won the 1988 architecture award; built around a large courtyard in traditional Arab design.

Dubai Museum
Displays the pre-oil history, located in Al Fahidi Fort.

Fujairah Old Town
Includes a 300-year old fort and ruins of old buildings.

Jumeirah Mosque
A medieval-style mosque with minarets and a golden central dome.

Sir Bani Yas
A major wildlife sanctuary.

Hatta Heritage Village
An ancient fortress village in foothills of the Hajar Mountains, with beautiful date palms and citrus orchards.

Sharjah Natural History Museum
Outstanding displays of desert life and "the living sea."

Qasr al Hosn
Built in 1793, this former ruler's residence is now a museum. It includes displays of Abu Dhabi's history and natural history.

Liwa Oasis
Forms the gateway to the Empty Quarter.

The Old Souq Area
Includes the Sharjah Heritage Museum and has shops selling such traditional items as pearls, perfumes, dates.

ABOUT THE CULTURE

NATIONAL HOLIDAY
National Day, December 2

LEADERS IN POLITICS
President Khalifa bin Zayid al-Nahyan; Prime Minister Muhammad bin Rashid al-Maktum

OFFICIAL NAME
United Arab Emirates

POPULATION
2,602,713 (2006)

CAPITAL
Abu Dhabi

ETHNIC GROUPS
Emirati 19 percent; other Arab and Iranian 23 percent; South Asians 50 percent; Westerners and East Asians 8 percent

LIFE EXPECTANCY
79 years for women, 76 years for men

RELIGIONS
Muslim 96 percent (Sunni 80 percent; Shia 16 percent); Christian and other 4 percent

LANGUAGES
Arabic (official), English, Persian, Hindi, Urdu

LITERACY RATE
77.9 percent

TIME LINE

IN UNITED ARAB EMIRATES	IN THE WORLD

5000–3000 B.C.
Evidence of human settlements
on coast and inland.

3000 B.C.
Region supplies copper to civilizations
in Mesopotamia.

2500–2000 B.C.
Maritime trade develops.

323 B.C.
Alexander the Great's empire stretches from
Greece to India.

A.D. 630–640
Islam comes to the region.

A.D. 700–900
Seafaring trade to India and China.

1000
The Chinese perfect gunpowder and
begin to use it in warfare.

1100
Rise of the Incan Civilization in Peru.

1206–1368
Genghis Khan unifies the Mongols and starts
conquest of the world. At its height, the Mongol
Empire under Kublai Khan stretches from China
to Persia and parts of Europe and Russia.

1500–1600
Portugal controls Persian Gulf trade.

1558–1603
Reign of Elizabeth I of England

1700–1800
Qawasim tribe of Ra's al-Khaymah controls
many Gulf ports.

1761
Abu Dhabi first settled.

1776
U.S. Declaration of Independence

1789–99
The French Revolution

1820
British forces attack Qawasim ports.
British sign the General Treaty of Peace
with the emirates.

1830–1840
Pearling industry thrives.

1833
Bani Yas tribe establishes Dubai, ruled by
the al-Maktoum family.

IN UNITED ARAB EMIRATES	IN THE WORLD
1853 The Perpetual Peace is signed, with the British providing protection to all the Trucial States.	**1861** The U.S. Civil War begins. **1869** The Suez Canal is opened. **1914** World War I begins.
1936–1952 Rulers of the Trucial States sign oil agreements with Western oil companies.	**1939** World War II begins. **1941** Japan attacks Pearl Harbor. **1945** The United States drops atomic bombs on Hiroshima and Nagasaki.
1959 Oil is discovered in Abu Dhabi.	**1949** The North Atlantic Treaty Organization (NATO) is formed.
1968 British announce plan to withdraw from the Gulf in 1971.	**1966–69** The Chinese Cultural Revolution.
1971 Britain withdraws from the Gulf. December 2: United Arab Emirates is formed.	
1973 OPEC (Organization of Petroleum Exporting Countries) quadruples crude oil prices.	
1979 OPEC again increases oil prices.	
1980 Iran-Iraq War.	**1986** Nuclear power disaster at Chernobyl in Ukraine
1990–1991 Iraq invades Kuwait; United States-led coalition defeats Iraq.	**1991** Breakup of the Soviet Union. **1997** Hong Kong is returned to China.
2001 UAE celebrates 30th anniversary of federation.	**2001** Terrorists crash planes in New York, Washington D.C., and Pennsylvania. **2003** War in Iraq begins.

GLOSSARY

aba
The traditional dress of Arab women.

barasti
The traditional house of the region's people, with a common room in front and a private room in the rear.

burka
A mask covering the nose and mouth, worn by Arab women.

dhow
The traditional boat of the Persian Gulf and much of Africa.

dishdash
The traditional, long garment or robe worn by Emerati men.

dugong
Also known as a sea cow—large, slow-moving sea mammals, related to the manatee of North America.

emir
A sheikh or ruler; source of the word emirate.

Emirati
The nationals of the United Arab Emirates.

falaj
The ancient system of irrigation, using stone-lined channels.

hajj
The Muslim pilgrimage to Mecca.

'Id al-fitr
The three- or four-day festival ending the Islamic month of Ramadan.

kahwa
Traditional UAE coffee.

Koran (or Qur'an)
The holy book of Islam.

majlis
The traditional communication between a sheikh and his subjects in which they are allowed to speak freely.

meze
An array of small dishes or dips served as appetizers in many UAE restaurants; a Lebanese tradition.

Rub' al-Khali
The Empty Quarter—the largest area of continuous desert in the world.

shamal
North and northwest winds that blow sand and dust off the desert in midwinter and early summer.

sharaf
The Bedu code of honor.

Trucial States
The unofficial union of the emirates formed by the Perpetual Truce, arranged by Great Britain.

FURTHER INFORMATION

BOOKS

Augustin, Byron. *United Arab Emirates*. Danbury, CT: Children's Press, 2002.

Davidson, Christopher M. *The United Arab Emirates: A Study in Survival*. Boulder, CO: Lynne Rienner Publications, 2005.

Editors of Explorer Publishing. *Images of Dubai and the United Arab Emirates*. Dubai, UAE: Explorer Publishing Co., 2002.

Hellyer, Peter, ed. *United Arab Emirates: A New Perspective*. London, UK: Trident Press, 2001.

WEB SITES

Official site of the UAE government. www.government.ae/gov/en/index.jsp

UAE Ministry of Information. www.uaeinteract.com/news

Central Intelligence Agency (CIA) World Factbook (Select UAE from country list). www.cia.gov/cia/publications/factbook/geos/ae.html

U.S. Department of State site, which includes background notes and major reports. www.state.gov/p/nea/ci/c2422.htm

BIBLIOGRAPHY

Camerapix. *United Arab Emirates*. Brooklyn, NY: Interlink Publishing Group, 2002.

Crocetti, Gina L. *Culture Shock! A Guide to Customs & Etiquette: United Arab Emirates*. Portland, OR Graphic Arts Center Publishing Co., 1997.

Forman, Werner and Michael Asher. *Phoenix Rising: The United Arab Emirates; Past, Present & Future*. London, UK: Harvill Press, 1996.

Kechichian, Joseph A., editor. *A Century in Thirty Years: Shaykh Zayed and the United Arab Emirates*. Middle East Policy Council, 2000.

Stannard, Dorothy, editor. *Insight Guide—Oman and the UAE*. New York: Langenscheidt Publishing Group, 1998.

INDEX